Stable Peace

*Sponsored by the Lyndon B. Johnson
School of Public Affairs*

Stable Peace
Kenneth E. Boulding

University of Texas Press, Austin & London

Library of Congress Cataloging in Publication Data

Boulding, Kenneth Ewart, 1910–
    Stable peace.
    1. Peace—Research. 2. International relations—
Research. I. Title.
JX1904.5.B69   327'.172'072   78-617
ISBN 0-292-76447-2
ISBN 0-292-76448-0 pbk.

Copyright © 1978 by the University of Texas Press

Set in Garamond Light by G & S Typesetters Inc.

Printed in the United States of America by

Edwards Brothers Inc.

Illustration by Ed Lindlof

Design by Richard Hendel

Contents

Preface

This book is a product of my tenure as the Distinguished Visiting Tom Slick Professor of World Peace at the Lyndon B. Johnson School of Public Affairs at the University of Texas in Austin during 1976–77. The first four chapters are essentially the substance of four public lectures I gave in the spring of 1977. The fifth chapter comes out of a seminar on peace research I gave in the fall of 1976. In the larger sense, of course, the book comes out of the forty years of thinking and writing which I have done in the field of war and peace, but it would not have crystallized, I suspect, if it had not been for my very enjoyable term as the Tom Slick Professor. I met Tom Slick once or twice in the late fifties and early sixties when we were both interested in the problems of peace research. I am not at all sure that he would have agreed with this little volume, but I like to think of it as a tribute to his memory. He was a very unusual man, of whom Texas should be very proud.

This book attempts to answer the question, If we had a policy for stable peace, what would it look like? Up to now peace has been regarded either as a utopian ideal or as something like the weather, over which we have no control. The desperate necessities of the nuclear age are forcing us to take peace seriously as an object of both personal and national policy. Policy, however, requires a theory to sustain it. We cannot, for instance, have an unemployment policy without some kind of theory of unemployment. The book begins, therefore, with a very brief and simple theory of war-peace systems in terms of a model of strain, strength (resistance to strain), and breaks, that is, the transition either from peace to war or from war to peace. I call this the chalk model—a piece of chalk breaks if the strain is too great for its strength. The difference between peace and war is mainly defined in terms of the taboo line—the line which divides what we can do but refrain from doing from what we can do and do. In peace we refrain from doing a great number of physically possible things which we do not refrain from doing in war, like bombing cities or invading territories.

The variables of war-peace systems, particularly the international system, can be classified roughly by the way in which they contribute either to the strain or to the strength of the system. Chapter 1 deals with the nature of these systems; chapter 2 with the dynamics of them. The concept of "causes of war" is rejected and we see war-peace systems as multicausal, subject to quite strong random influences and to sharp discontinuities at the breaking points. Chapter 3 on the justice of peace is devoted to an extremely important, special variable which affects both the strain and the strength: the perceptions of justice of the system in particular times and places.

Besides the particular phases of the system of war and

peace, which are fairly sharply distinguished, general phases of the system are identified, particularly stable war, unstable war, unstable peace, and stable peace. Stable peace is the object of peace policy. It is a phase of the system in which the strength is sufficiently larger than the strain, so that the inevitably cyclical and random movements within the system never carry us over the boundary into war. There is a long, painful, slow but very persistent historical movement from stable war into unstable war into unstable peace into stable peace. The main object of peace policy is to speed up the transition by deliberate decision.

Prediction in systems of this kind is extremely difficult because of the strong importance of random factors and of undetectable discontinuities. Fortunately policy does not demand prediction. It demands merely changes in the parameters of the system which make peace more probable and war less probable. In chapter 4 a number of types of policy directed toward this end are suggested: (1) a declaration of intent to pursue a peace policy, and the setting up of organizations within a government to pursue it and monitor it; (2) the development of Graduated and Reciprocated Initiative in Tension-Reduction (GRIT), as proposed by Professor Charles Osgood; (3) the development of strategies and organizations for nonviolent change and resistance to unwanted change; (4) the development of appropriate international governmental organizations; (5) the encouragement of appropriate international nongovernmental organizations; (6) the encouragement and development of research in the whole area of peace and conflict management, including the study of the impact of policy in such other areas as population development, distribution, and so on, which may affect the success of peace policy. The book concludes with a chapter on the present status of research for peace and suggestions for its improvement.

What this book is proposing is neither utopia nor certainty. The problem of peace policy is seen not as how to achieve immediate and certain success but as how to introduce a bias into the system that moves it toward stable peace at a more rapid rate. Policy is social agriculture: just as a farmer both cooperates with and distorts the ecosystem of the farm in the interest of certain human values, so the policy maker must cooperate with and distort the overall dynamics of society. The peace policy proposed here is practical and achieveable. It is important to recognize, however, that it is not now being pursued and that the policies which are now being pursued are far more dangerous to the human race and inimical to human values than the policies here proposed.

Stable Peace

1. The meaning of peace

Peace is a word of so many meanings that one hesitates to use it for fear of being misunderstood. When, for instance, a group of us started the Center for Research on Conflict Resolution at the University of Michigan in 1956, we conceived it as a center for peace research, but we deliberately avoided the use of the word "peace" in the title because of the misunderstandings which might arise. The concept of peace has both positive and negative aspects. On the positive side, peace signifies a condition of good management, orderly resolution of conflict, harmony associated with mature relationships, gentleness, and love. On the negative side, it is conceived as the absence of something—the absence of turmoil, tension, conflict, and war.

These contrasting aspects of the concept are likewise reflected in a certain ambiguity with regard to the evaluation of peace. Like every other aspect of life, our evaluation of peace or its opposites depends on how much we have. There is a universal law of diminishing marginal utility which says that every virtue becomes a vice if there is too much of it and that our evaluation of all particular goods tends to diminish as their quantity increases. We all appreciate the tranquility of a calm summer evening or a Constable landscape. Still, as W. S. Gilbert says, "There is beauty in the bellow of the blast, There is grandeur in the growling of the gale."[1] Tranquility derives part of its charm from contrast with a preceding storm.

A negative evaluation of peace is reflected in certain connotations of words like pacify, pacification, and appeasement, all of which are derived from the Latin word for peace (*pax, pacis*). To pacify is to calm down childish behavior. A generation or so ago it was an almost universal custom to put something called a pacifier in a baby's mouth when he or she cried. I am sure there are many places where this is still done. Pacification can easily be a synonym for ruthless military oppression. Appeasement has had a bad name ever since Neville Chamberlain and the supposed appeasement of Hitler. On an even more negative set of values, peace is rated with death. After all, we do put "rest in peace" on tombstones, although W. C. Fields is supposed to have wanted to put "on the whole I would rather be in Philadelphia" on his tombstone. The peace of emptiness, making a desert and calling it peace (Tacitus), the peace of mind that is a withdrawal from reality, the peace of the catatonic trance have much in common with the peace of death. It is not surprising that we are suspicious of these negative forms of peace. The human race has often put a high value on struggle, strife, turmoil, excitement. We identify vigor with stress, with triumph. Our sports ritualize the value of striving in

1. W. S. Gilbert, *The Mikado*.

what I have called a ritual dialectic, in which winning is valued for its own sake. Perhaps the greatest enemy of peace is the perception that it is dull.

On the other hand, there is a high valuation of the positive concept of peace, which is seen as a skill in the management of conflict and the development of a larger order than that which involves warring parties. The opposite of this kind of peace is then seen as a clearly pathological state of some kind of war. War or "not-peace" involves the inability to manage conflict, to the cost of both parties. It involves disruptive dialectic, unnecessary confusion, childish quarreling, immaturity of political form. Peace in this larger, more positive sense is quite consistent with conflict and excitement, debate and dialogue, drama and confrontation. But it provides a setting within which these processes do not get out of hand, become pathological, and cause more trouble than they are worth. In this sense of the word, peace is one of the ultimate time's arrows in the evolutionary process, an increasing product of human development and learning. This is close to a religious sense of the word peace, the sense in which Saint Francis prays, "Make me an instrument of Thy peace," or Dante writes, "in His will is our peace."

In all the major religions there is also a transcendental concept of peace. It is particularly strong in Christianity. This is the "My peace I give unto you: not as the world giveth" of Jesus[2] and the "peace of God, which passeth all understanding."[3] There is something of this perhaps in the concept of nirvana in Buddhism, though this

2. John 14:27.
3. Philippians 4:7.

sometimes looks dangerously like the peace of death. A "peace which passeth all understanding" is perhaps hard to do research on, but there is a large record of human experience that this means something, and it is translated into the behavior of martyrs and those who have suffered for their faith with equanimity and calm forgiveness.

While this larger, more transcendent concept of peace underlies a great deal of the anguished search for it throughout human history, it is peace in a narrower sense which is easier to understand, more susceptible to specific research, and more susceptible also to recommendations for policy. In what follows, therefore, I propose to concentrate mainly on the concept of peace as the absence of war. This is not such a negative concept as might appear at first sight, as we can regard both peace and war as alternating phases or conditions of the relationship between social entities, particularly political entities. The relationship between any two social entities —whether individuals, families, churches, tribes, businesses, nation-states, provinces, even regions—can usually be identified and its position described on some scale that has peace at one end and war at the other. When we do this, we find that while there may be a few doubtful cases in the middle—not quite peace and not quite war—we also find an overwhelming clustering either at the peace end of the scale or the war end.

With some social institutions the condition of peace is so overwhelmingly common that we hardly ever think of war at all. Most families, for instance, live at peace with their neighboring families. They may quarrel and litigate and still be at peace. Sometimes, however, the relationship between families does break down into something that can be called war, as in the vendetta and the feud. The McCoys and the Hatfields traditionally had a relationship which clearly deserved the name of interfamilial war. Businesses, again, are almost universally at peace with each other. There have been occasional times in history when, for example, the East India Company was at war with corresponding companies from other countries, but then the business is acting like a political state. Churches, likewise, are rarely at war with other churches, though it is not uncommon for a state to be at war with a church, as in the persecutions of the early Christians and, indeed, of almost all religions in their early stages. There are, of course, wars of religion, but these take place primarily when the church becomes aligned to some political body, though sometimes it is not easy to say where the church ends and the state begins.

War is much commoner between political organizations than between any other kind of social organization. Indeed, one sometimes has the feeling that for political organizations war is almost a norm—peace is the exception. Bands, tribes, city-states, nations, and empires are very frequently at war with each other. Nevertheless, even in this case there is a condition of peace and, if we ask knowledgeable historians of a period whether country A was at peace or at war with country B on a given date, they will usually be able to answer. There may be some ambiguous cases, such as the early involvement of the United States in Vietnam, guerrilla activity, the cold war, and so on. Ordinarily, however, war is a distinct pattern of behavior very different from behavior under conditions of peace. Frequently the transition from peace to war is signalized by some ritual act such as a declaration of war, and the transition from war to peace is signalized by an armistice or a treaty. Nowadays these ritual acts seem to be becoming increasingly uncommon because of the delegitimation of war in the modern world. An undeclared war, however, can be as readily identified as war as a declared war. It is sometimes a little difficult to point to the exact moment of transition, but it can usually be pinpointed within a relatively short interval of time.

Both war and peace are positively definable states of a system, each with a characteristic set of properties. Neither is merely the absence of the other. Similarly, being asleep and being awake are two different states with different behavioral and descriptive properties. Neither is simply the opposite of the other. Here again there may be certain transition states of being half-awake, but these are rather rare—most people can identify the times in the past twenty-four hours, let us say, when they have been awake and when they have been asleep. In this sense, therefore, both war and peace can be regarded as alternating states of the larger system of the interrelationship of what might be called warring parties. The total pattern of relationship over time might be called a war-peace system.

The war-peace system is often confused with the structure of conflict and nonconflict. The relationship is illustrated in figure 1. Human activities can be divided into conflictual activities and nonconflictual activities. Here again there may be a middle ground where the classification is in doubt, but all important sets are fuzzy. Nonconflict includes such things as eating, drinking, sleeping, working, procreating, reading, learning, walking, traveling, and so on. It constitutes by far the larger

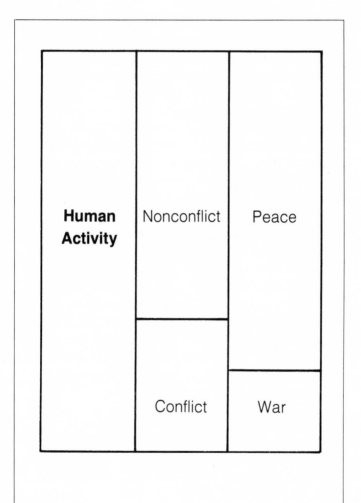

1. The structure of conflict and nonconflict

proportion of the activities of the human race. Conflict activities are those in which we are conscious that an increase in our welfare may diminish the welfare of others or an increase in the welfare of others may diminish our welfare.[4]

Thus, conflict is a redistributional situation where there is gain for some and loss for others. The distinction between war and peace is not quite the same as that between conflict and nonconflict. All nonconflict is peace, but conflict can be divided into war and peace, depending on the nature of the taboos involved. In peaceful conflicts, each party's taboos impose sharp limitations on the amount of damage each party is permitted to do to the other. In games, for instance, it is rare for one party to poison the other. In democratic elections, likewise, there is frequently no physical violence of one party or candidate against the other. When there is, the situation is edging from peace into war. In international war, on the other hand, there are virtually no limits to the violence one party can inflict upon the other, and almost all taboos are dissolved. We can summarize the relationship by saying that all war involves conflict,

4. In the language of the theory of games, this might be called the redistributional game. It is not quite the same as the zero-sum game, in which an increase in the welfare of A is equal to a diminution in the welfare of B, for there are positive-sum games (in which there is an increase in the total welfare of both parties) which are redistributional, in the sense that the gain to one party is definitely a loss for the other. Thus, suppose we have a situation in which A's gain is $+5$ and B's is -3. It is a positive-sum game but is still redistributional. Zero-sum games and negative-sum games must be redistributional. In a zero-sum game, if A's gain is $+5$, B's must be -5. In the negative-sum game, A gains and B loses more than A gains.

some conflict involves peace, and all nonconflict involves peace.

We now need to get an image in our mind of the total world system which we are studying. Studies of war and peace tend to concentrate so much on particular episodes that it is not easy to get a sense of the total picture. Let us imagine, then, a map of the world big enough so each of the 4 billion human beings can be represented by a dot. This will have to be about 1 mile by 2 miles! We can color the dots according to the degree to which each person is engaged in actual acts of violence during a particular day. Dots representing persons engaged in killings, bombings, destruction, and so on we color a bright red. Then we color the dots pink that represent people who are preparing for potential violence, even though they may not actually be engaged in it on this day. This will include all the armed forces of the world and the associated war industries. It may also include gangsters, criminals, and police in varying degrees. Perhaps we color orange those dots representing persons engaged in nonviolent conflict: organizers, demonstrators, lawyers, court officials, arbitrators, negotiators, collective bargainers, and so on. And the rest of the dots representing people engaged in nonconflictual occupations can be colored blue. This will be the vast mass of the human race engaged in education, manufacture, travel, innumerable leisure activities, and so on. Suppose we now reduce this large map so the individual dots are no longer visible but merge into colors, with some areas perhaps bright red, trailing off into various tones of blue. Suppose we now make a similar transparent map for every day of human history and we pile these in the correct order of the days, so we have an enormous transparent cuboid. We will then have an image of human violence as it spreads out through time and space. In such a three-dimensional map a war will appear as an irregular red or purplish cylinder, something like a worm, running along the time dimension through a varying cross section or sequence of maps.

If we now take any particular area and follow it back through time on our three-dimensional map, we may find four patterns. First, we may find periods when the map is continuously red, or at least reddish purple, where war is virtually incessant. Really bright red spots —the battles, the air raids, and so on—will actually be fairly rare, but there will be periods in which the overall color is reddish purple. Second, we may find other periods in which the worm of time is striped, with alternating periods of war and relative peace. On the map this is like stripes of reddish purple and bluish purple. In some cases the periods of war may predominate. This is what I have called unstable war, the situation in which war is regarded as the norm but is interrupted by periods of relative peace. The actual proportions of war and peace would not necessarily be a sufficient indicator of this condition, though there would undoubtedly be a tendency for a condition of unstable war to produce periods with a larger proportion of times of war. The critical problem here is whether war or peace is regarded as the norm.

We might find a third condition, also striped, but in which the periods of peace were longer, which might be described as unstable peace. This is the condition in which peace is regarded as the norm and war is regarded as a breakdown of peace, which will be restored when the war is over. Then, finally, we might find periods of stable peace, of a fairly solid blue, though with a little purplish cast if there are organized preparations for a war which never comes. Stable peace is a situation in which the probability of war is so small that it does not really enter into the calculations of any of the people involved.

In order to bring our map of the world closer to the immense complexities of reality, we should indicate the character of the interrelationships among the dots which represent the 4 billion human beings. These interrelationships are, of course, of many kinds: there is a vast network of exchange relationships which, together with the production and consumption going on with each individual, constitute the major structure of economic life. We will find conflictual relationships, either peaceful or warring; we will find relationships of communication, instructions, orders and ideas, works of art or literature, telegrams, letters and books, orders of the day. We will find communications from the past in the form of written records and artifacts coming through the time dimension of our transparent cuboid. We will find patterns of networks—for instance, hierarchical patterns in the communications network look something like a root system, starting at the top of the hierarchy and working down through successive layers. And we will find intimate groups where everybody communicates with everyone else.

We can color these lines between the dots as we have colored the dots themselves: blue for nonconflict relations, running from bluish purple into reddish purple, into pink and into bright red, as the relationships move through peaceful conflict into war. We might even denote the intensity of the relationship by the thickness of the lines. We end up on a map of the world with a vast spiderweb of red, blue, and purple lines. A lot of the red dots will have blue lines connecting them, such as members of the same army, and red lines will connect them with members of other armies. In earlier days, the networks will cluster into a large number of isolated webs. A thousand years ago, for instance, we will see isolated webs in the Andes, in Mexico, in Europe, in India, in Japan, and so on. As we move forward in time, the connecting lines will increase along with the number of dots, until today we have a network that covers the whole world, even though some portions are denser than others.

As the world becomes more interconnected, so war becomes more interconnected. A thousand years ago a war in the Americas would have no connection whatever with a war in India or a war in Europe. These wars would represent completely independent systems, though they might follow much the same general pattern, simply because they are part of the human race. Two hundred years ago wars in America were closely connected with wars in Europe, though there were probably wars in central Africa that were not connected with Europe. Even today violence in Northern Ireland has very little to do with violence in Cyprus or in Lebanon, though there are thin connecting lines between these places. This is a system of such vast complexity that we tend to fall into two opposite traps regarding it: we either throw up our hands in despair, giving up all attempts to understand the system, going back to folk knowledge, superstition, and myth, or we attempt so drastic an over-simplification, as both the Marxists and the national decision makers often do, that our mental map of the system becomes so inaccurate that it leads us into severe mistakes.

As we try to describe the system more exactly, we have to recognize that each of these 4 billion dots is an individual human being of immense complexity, and we have to try to describe what is relevant to the problem of war and peace. Blue dots and red dots will be alike in many important respects, different in other respects, but we have to ask ourselves, what is the essential difference between a warring party and a nonwarring party? The basic answer to this question would seem to be found in the nature of the taboo system of the parties involved. Every person at any moment in time has a range of possible behaviors and actions. The range of physically possible behaviors is quite large: we may go up on a roof and jump off or plunge our table knife into the heart of our dinner companion. We do not even consider these possibilities because they are beyond what might be called the taboo line; that is, they are things which could physically be done but which are beyond our psychological barrier. But from the point of view of the warring party the transition from peace to war is largely a transition in the position of the taboo line. There is a whole range of actions which are taboo in peace but which are not taboo in war.

In the description of the taboo system, therefore, the description of the self-image of the parties involved is of the utmost importance. It determines their behavior and particularly determines their taboos: what people do not do is just as important as what they do do. Thus, the Ford Motor Company might be experiencing severe competition from General Motors but, if it ever occurred to the directors of the Ford Motor Company to assassinate the directors of General Motors and blow up their plant, it is very doubtful whether that thought would even have been expressed in a board meeting, simply because the self-image of the Ford Motor Company would not permit that kind of behavior even if it were physically possible. Self-images, of course, change under stress, and they likewise erode and change under a lack of stress. Husbands and wives, for instance, not infrequently quarrel, not infrequently make each other miserable, but the murder of one spouse by another is really quite rare (even though it is one of the commonest types of murder), simply because normally the self-image of a spouse does not include the self-image of a murderer. Occasionally, however, stress rises to the point where the self-image crosses that terrible boundary, the taboo line shifts, and the appropriate behavior is tragically likely to follow.

In the case of nation-states, the self-image of the state as a potential war maker is so common as to be almost universal, though there are some interesting exceptions in those areas that can be described as stable peace. Thus, in the self-image of the United States in the minds of its decision makers, the idea of a military invasion of Canada is so far below the mental horizon as to be almost, though not quite, nonexistent, and the same goes for the decision makers of Canada. Here the national images are mutually compatible, the border is disarmed, and the probability of war is extremely low. The same could be said of the relations of the United States and Great Britain, at least after sometime in the late nineteenth century. I recall, as a young man in the mid-1930s, a conference on British agriculture near London at which the question was raised as to whether Britain should try to be more self-sufficient in foodstuffs in light of a possible future war, which at that time was looming on the horizon, and I recall a tired British voice from a high-placed official saying, "If we are at war with America, we can't get our food; if we are not at war with America, we can get our food; we shall never be at war with America, why don't we change the subject?" It was a remarkable revelation to me at least of the fact that the British government had a self-image in which the probability of war with America was zero.

The stable peace relationship is not the same thing as having a common language, a common religion, a common culture, or even common interests. The common language and similar culture of Great Britain and the United States certainly did not prevent the War of 1812 or the American Revolution. The common language, culture, and religion of the Spanish-speaking countries of Latin America, for instance, have never prevented them from fighting each other, and indeed their wars have been singularly bloody.[5] Neither similarities nor differences are any guarantee of peace, though they are not irrelevant and must be seen as part of the larger picture. The only guarantees of peace are compatible self-images. These have been produced largely, one suspects, by accident, though occasionally by an almost subconscious series of policies.

A problem here, as we shall see in more detail later, is that each party in a relationship tends to create the self-image of the other in a very complex, mutual learning process. To a distressing extent each party in a conflict-

5. Lewis F. Richardson, *Statistics of Deadly Quarrels* (Pittsburgh: Boxwood Press, 1960).

ual relationship is a creation of its enemies. In some
degree Napoleon created Bismarck, Bismarck created
Clemenceau, Clemenceau created Hitler, Hitler created
the Pentagon, Stalin created the CIA. Perhaps one reason for the biblical injunction to love our enemies is that
they make us. One of the critical questions is, what can
break this cycle? It is a real puzzler. One is tempted to
formulate a kind of law of social entropy which says
that the natural order of things is for everything to go
from bad to worse. Folly, illusion, and ill will in one
party produce a greater folly, illusion, and ill will in
another, and this feeds back to produce still greater
folly, illusion, and ill will in the first party, and so on in
an ever increasing spiral that can only end in catastrophe.

On the more optimistic side, however, there seems to
be another process at work, though it is less well understood. It is akin to the larger processes of evolution in
which learning proceeds and knowledge and knowhow
increase. There is at least some evidence both from biological evolution and from human history that these
long, slow processes of learning of skills, though they
may only be able to take place as it were in the cracks in
the system, are so persistent that they eventually prevail
in spite of the tendency for rising social entropy in many
of the structured parts of the system. This is one meaning perhaps of the poetic and religious insight that "His
will is our peace." It is very hard to describe this learning process precisely in terms of our simple map. Nevertheless, it is something very real. I was convinced of this
when, in the middle of the Watergate episode, I happened to see *Macbeth*. It occurred to me that *Macbeth*
was Watergate, only a thousand years earlier and a

thousand years bloodier, and that there has been a social and political learning process in the interval.

One of the sources of hope is precisely the fact that beyond a certain threshold war tends to alternate with peace. These transitions are quite sharp. The United States was at war with Japan in 1944; it is not at war with Japan today. Neither is the United States at war with the Soviet Union, in spite of the serious conflict between them. A cold war is peace not war, even though it may not be very high quality peace and it may be unstable. Two countries at peace may spy on each other, impose various restrictions, put tariffs on each other's goods, have an arms race, prepare plans for each other's destruction, but as long as they are at peace they do not carry out these plans. In peace, indeed, there are certain taboos: countries do not bomb each other's cities; they do not invade each other; though they may mass their armies on each other's borders, they do not cross these borders; they do not sink each other's ships. In war these taboos are removed. The transition from peace to war is a sharp and discontinuous movement of the taboo line, that is, the boundary which divides the things the self-image permits to be done from the things it does not permit to be done.

Even in war there is a vestigial taboo line. There are laws of war which are quite frequently observed with regard to the treatment of prisoners, the use of certain weapons, and so on. In the Second World War, for instance, neither party used poison gas though each had it. These taboos, however, are precarious and, especially under the stress of impending defeat, it is easy for the taboo line of war to be moved to allow practices which previously were not allowed. We see this particularly if we contrast the wars of the eighteenth century with the wars of the twentieth century. On the whole, the former were fought by semiprofessional, lower-class soldiers directed by professional, upper-class generals and states-men, and the destruction was frequently quite limited by taboos which both sides observed. In twentieth-century war these taboos have largely been removed, and there is wholesale slaughter of civilians. Part of this perhaps is the development of unfamiliar weapons, for which the taboos have not yet been established. Part of it also is the essential fragility of taboos in the war situation itself.

An aspect of reality which is hard to put onto our map but which is of great importance, particularly in those decisions which lead to a transition from war to peace or from peace to war, is the structure of decision making and power. Some of the human beings on our map obviously have much more power than others in the sense that their decisions affect the condition and be-havior of large numbers of others. This has a good deal to do with the nature of the hierarchical structure and the communications structure. Powerful people tend to be at the top of hierarchies and to have complex struc-tures of communication emanating from them. There is a myth that war is an activity of the whole nation and that the whole nation decides to make the transition from peace to war or from war to peace. This, however, is very unrealistic because of the concentrations of po-litical power. In all nations, even in democratic societies, the decision-making power with regard to war and peace is highly concentrated, though it is always to some ex-tent modified by the fear of possible consequences to the decision maker. In monarchical societies the monarchs, of course, have the power to declare war and to make peace, though this power may be limited by the fear they may have of the consequences of these decisions, either to themselves or to their family, associates, friends, or even the whole country, toward which they may feel some sense of stewardship. The extent to which President Johnson was able to involve the United States in a war in Vietnam without any formal declaration by Congress suggests that, at least with regard to the international system, the United States is a good deal more like a monarchy than is commonly supposed. Here again the principle of being created by enemies seems to hold, for the powers of the president of the United States undoubtedly exceed those of George III at the time of the American Revolution! It is ironic that the American Revolution seems to have produced a much more monarchical society in the United States than it did in Great Britain, which was a limited oligarchy in 1776 and has moved toward a somewhat less limited oligarchy in the intervening two hundred years.

Unfortunately, it is hard to derive any strong general principles about describing and classifying the transitions from peace to war or from war to peace because these are what might be called threshold decisions, and it is always very hard to say what determines the threshold. Before war begins, there is almost invariably a period of rising tension. There may be some exceptions to this in carefully planned wars of surprise, where the intentions of the aggressor are kept secret up to the very moment of attack, but these are rather rare. We can think of a prewar period as one in which the probability of war gradually rises, until one day the dice register "war" and the fatal decision is made. There is a fairly strong random element in all complex decision making, especially by powerful people.

What we have in the international system, therefore, is something not unlike the system of the earth's atmosphere, in which certain probabilities develop but the actual course of the weather depends on largely random circumstances at any particular time. This view of the world is resisted quite strongly because the human race seems to have a great intolerance for randomness, particularly with regard to things that are close and important to us. It is for this reason that we constantly tend to fall into superstition, which is the perception of order in situations where there really is none. Superstition indeed is an attempt to rationalize randomness. We see this particularly in political superstition, which is almost universal. People like to believe in conspiracies and subtle causes—economic, psychological, diabolical, or something. We find it very hard to recognize the fact that in many systems the random element is quite strong.

Another parallel to the transitions from war to peace or from peace to war would be automobile accidents. If we have automobiles, there is a positive probability that in a given period a certain number of us will run into each other. War is a kind of automobile accident of the international system. With a given set of capabilities and drivers, certain probabilities perhaps can be established, though exactly when and where the accident takes place is something with a strong random element. The parallel breaks down, of course, because in the international system there are not very many automobiles, and one drunken driver in such a situation can create a fairly predictable amount of damage. But the principle remains that the search for "meaning" in a particular war is often futile. The war in Vietnam was a good example. We could trace it to a set of unlucky decisions, any one of which could have gone the other way with a certain probability. The illusion of necessity, however, often imposes itself on the system, for this is a case where expectations are often self-justified. If two nations expect to go to war with each other, the probability that they will do so is thereby considerably raised. If they do not expect to go to war with each other, the probability that they will do so is correspondingly lowered.

An additional complexity in the system is the interaction of the dynamics of domestic processes within nations with the dynamics of their international relations. The connection is looser than is often thought. The international system certainly has a dynamic of its own which is frequently rather independent of what is happening inside the respective nations. It is rarely true, for instance, that we have arms races in order to solve domestic unemployment problems or that war is a deliberate attempt to create national unity in the face of some sort of national internal disintegration. That factors such as these play an occasional role is likely, but the view that they play a dominant or determining role is another example of political superstition.

The theory that war and peace are determined by conflicts of economic interest is particularly untenable. The pattern of economic interest is not easy to describe on our world map, but it almost certainly has a shape very different from the pattern of war and peace. Economic interest is an extremely complex matrix which cuts across almost all organized or self-conscious groups such as classes or nations. Any action or policy theoretically divides the human race into three interest groups: those who are favorably affected, those who are unfavorably affected, and those who are unaffected. These three groups, however, usually cut across all conscious units and rarely correspond to any organization, class, nation, religion, or self-conscious group.

Occupational groups come closest to being interest groups, and of these the most significant from the point of view of war and peace are the military themselves and the war industry that supplies them. The rise of the war industry to a substantial proportion of national economies, which has only really taken place in the last hundred years, is an important new factor in the incidence of war and peace and in the transitions between war and peace, but it is by no means easy to assess its impact. Bruce Russett, for instance, did a study which showed that the hawks in the United States Congress did not generally come from those districts and states in which the war industry was heavily located and that there was no statistical relationship—possibly even a negative one—between the proportion of the congressional district or state economy devoted to the war industry and the warlikeness of the representatives and senators.[6] Whatever effect there is is completely overlaid by the fact that the war industry is concentrated in the more industrialized sectors, which tend to produce more sophisticated representatives and senators. There does seem to be a fairly strong relationship between rural people and militarism, perhaps because there is some-

6. Bruce Russett, *What Price Vigilance? The Burdens of National Defense* (New Haven: Yale University Press, 1970), pp. 56–90.

thing about closeness to the land which produces a consciousness of territoriality.

For any two nations, for any given period of time, it is fairly easy to measure what proportion of time is spent in war and what proportion is spent in peace. The statistical study of the incidence of war and peace was pioneered by Lewis Richardson in his famous *Statistics of Deadly Quarrels*. Attempts to find correlates of this incidence, however, have been frustratingly disappointing. For instance, Professor Rudi Rummel's studies of the dimensionality of nations, while they have employed the most sophisticated statistical methods, have failed to come up with any clear correlates of the incidence of war and peace.[7] The studies by Vern Bullough and Raoul Naroll[8] of the incidence of war in a historical sample of societies all over the world cast grave doubt on the old adage that, if you want peace, you should prepare for war, for most societies prepared for war seem to get it, which is not wholly surprising. On the other hand, correlates on the incidence of peace are elusive. Royal marriages seem to help, but even that relationship is pretty loose, and one is tempted to conclude that at least over the world of the last five thousand years or so the best way to have peace is to be lucky and to be in a geographical and social situation in which the integrative forces are stronger than the disintegrative ones.

Another very large set of data which we really ought

7. Rudi J. Rummel, *The Dimensions of Nations* (Beverly Hills: Sage Publications, 1972).
8. Vern Bullough and Raoul Naroll, *Deterrence in History* (New York: State University of New York Press, 1969).

to put onto our world map (we would probably have to enlarge it to do so) is the location of stocks and items of human artifacts of all kinds. A set of human artifacts which is particularly relevant to problems of war and peace is weaponry, though stocks of food, clothing, shelter, and means of transport are by no means irrelevant, as armies have to be fed, clothed, sheltered, and moved. These artifacts change over time. The impact of technical change in weaponry on the nature and the incidence of war and peace has been great, though the effects have often been extremely complex. A new weapon or a new form of military organization, like Alexander's army, may produce the rise and eventual fall of empires. I have argued that the range of the deadly missile is one of the most important variables affecting the size of warring parties for, the larger the range of the missile, the larger must be the minimum viable size of the warring party.[9]

With arrows and spears, city-states and feudal barons were viable within their city or castle walls. The invention of gunpowder, by substantially increasing the range of the deadly missile, virtually destroyed the viability of both the feudal baron and the city-state, though the latter has a tendency to revive under circumstances of what might be called conditional viability, like Singapore or Hong Kong or even Monaco, which a larger unit could wipe out but chooses not to. The development of the guided missile and the nuclear warhead, however, confronts the human race with a quite unprecedented problem, for it has destroyed unconditional viability of even

9. Kenneth E. Boulding, *Conflict and Defense: A General Theory* (New York: Harper, 1962).

the largest countries. When the range of a deadly missile rises to 12,500 miles, or half the circumference of the earth, it is clear that a fundamental watershed has been passed and that war itself is no longer a viable institution.

One virtue of thinking of the world as a great three-dimensional map in space and time is that it may help save us from two major fallacies. The first great fallacy is our tendency to divide the world into two and only two parts. This dichotomous thinking always overlooks the multiplicity of the world and the extreme complexity of its interrelationships. This plagues our thinking even about war and peace, which certainly look dichotomous enough. The second fallacy is our failure to perceive the quantities and proportions of the system. Our attention is so heavily concentrated on things which are unusual, visual, and spectacular that we tend to overestimate the importance of these things. We have already noticed, for instance, that, while war and peace are phases of conflictual behavior, nonconflictual behavior is of far greater quantitative importance. Conflictual behavior, indeed, has to be seen as a kind of brightly colored periphery of a great, rather commonplace mass of nonconflictual behavior. Even when two countries are at war, a large part of the behavior of the inhabitants is totally unrelated to the war—sleeping, eating, making love, having children, producing civilian goods, and so on. It is true that there has been a rise in the proportion of the activity of society devoted to war as societies have gotten richer and been able to afford it. Adam Smith says, "Among the civilized nations of modern Europe, not more than one hundredth part of the inhabitants of any country can be employed as soldiers without ruin to the country that pays the expense of their service."[10] In the Second World War, the contending parties devoted over 40 percent of the gross national product to the war. The gross national product, however, represents only a fraction of total human behavior—not more than a quarter —so in terms of behavior the greatest war effort in human history is probably not more than 10 percent of the total behavior even of the contending parties and is a much smaller proportion of the behavior of the whole human race. In earlier periods the overall impact of war was much smaller.

Over the course of human history, the chance of dying in a war has really been quite small. Even in the belligerent twentieth century, the total number of human deaths must have been about 1½ to 2 billion. Practically all the people who were alive in 1900 are now dead, as well as a considerable proportion of those born since. All the wars of the twentieth century to date did not kill more than about 80 million people, or about 4 percent of the total number of deaths. The proportion of premature deaths caused through war would, of course, be larger—that is, deaths before old age—but one doubts if it could be more than 10 percent. The destruction of property by war, also, must be compared with the depreciation which goes on all the time. This is even harder to estimate than the proportion of deaths due to war, but I would be surprised even in the twentieth century if the destruction of human artifacts, buildings, machines, goods of all kinds, and so on directly due to war were

10. Adam Smith, *The Wealth of Nations*, Modern Library Edition (New York: Random House, 1937), pp. 657–658.

more than 5 percent of capital depreciation. Even in advanced societies, for instance, the total capital stock is of the order of three or four years' total income. This means in effect that total capital stock is destroyed on an average of every four years, though some items, of course, survive very much longer.

The losses due to war are of two kinds. There is the highly visible destruction of life and of goods, of which we are highly aware. On the other hand are the unborn and the unmade, that is, the human beings who do not come into existence because of the decline of birth rates due to war and the goods which are not made because of the resources absorbed by the war industry. In terms of the impact of the war on human population, the numbers of the unborn may actually outweigh the numbers of those killed, though this was probably not true in the Second World War. The quantity of unborn goods —that is, the houses and hospitals, factories, and consumer goods of all kinds which were not made because of the energy devoted to the war industry, both in peace and in war—far exceeds the actual destruction due to war itself. This has been particularly true since the Second World War. The actual wars in this period have been fairly small, sporadic, and quite localized. The actual damage they have done is a very small proportion of the total world output for this period. On the other hand, in this period the world war industry has probably averaged something like 6 to 10 percent or perhaps even more of the total world product. Summing this over thirty years means that the human race has lost at least two full years, perhaps more, of its total product, which might have been devoted to making everybody richer.

These are essentially the economic costs of the system of deterrence and they are very high, even though deterrence may produce an unstable peace.

In the past, therefore, we could think of the world as consisting of a small war-peace segment of human activity and a much larger productive segment that planted, reaped, made, consumed, enjoyed, appreciated, and so on. My terminology admittedly is a little contentious. Some would argue that the war-peace segment of human activity is the only dramatic, exciting, and interesting part of it and that the drama, excitement, and interest it produces may be worth the cost in human lives and goods. This is an argument that has been taken seriously. An economist, however, is always interested in how to get things cheap and, particularly in this case, how to get satisfaction from drama, struggle, conflict, dialectics, and so on at a lower cost in lives and goods. Furthermore, the world has changed on us. Up to the present time the war-peace segment of human activity has been relatively small and has not seriously interfered with human development on the whole, though it has done so in particular times and in particular places. We now face a situation in which the war-peace sector of human activity tends to expand cancerously and actively threaten the productive sector, even to the point where the evolutionary drama on this planet might come to an end. The problem of controlling the war-peace sector, therefore, is becoming of overriding importance to human survival. This sector can no longer be regarded as a minor aberration of human development, and the problem of controlling it has become of the first priority.

2. The sources of peace

In a system as complex as the one we have been describing, the concept of cause and effect in any simple sense is of very dubious value. For one thing, the system has strong random elements; it is partly indeterminate. It cannot be described in any terms as simple as the equations of celestial mechanics. Small causes sometimes produce large effects, large causes small effects. The system is full of thresholds and discontinuities, and any attempt to present it as a simple determinate system is a violation of reality. Nevertheless, it is not all chaos. It has strong nonrandom structures as well as randomness, and it is the business of science to perceive nonrandomness and to detect its patterns.

What we are looking for is something like a phase theory. We perceive in the war-peace system at least two sets of structures. One is the alternation of peace and war, each of which represents a different phase of a relationship and alternative clusters or patterns of behavior. These might be called the special phases of the system. We are particularly interested in the underlying conditions which generate the transition either from peace to war or from war to peace as well as the sort of behavior which characterizes each condition of the system. We are looking for something that might be called a transition probability function, with the probability of the transition from peace to war if the system is at peace, or from war to peace if the system is at war, expressed as a function dependent on certain other characteristics of the system. We seek, also, useful categories of these other characteristics.

Besides the special phases of the system of war and peace we also have, as we saw in the last chapter, general phases—descriptive of the overall likelihood or distribution of war and peace in the system—which could be described as stable war, unstable war, unstable peace, and stable peace. We are also looking for characteristics and descriptions of the system which help determine in which of these general phases the system will find itself.

It is possible to lump most of the characteristics of these systems under two general headings, which we might call strain and strength. Under the heading of strain, we put those elements of the system that are particularly conducive to phase change—in this case from peace to war or from war to peace. It may not be possible to put an exact aggregate measure on strain, for it is a group of somewhat heterogeneous factors. Nevertheless, it is a property of the system which is clearly subject to qualitative estimation and which we can talk about in the ordinal terms of "more" or "less."

Similarly, there is a cluster of properties of social systems which might be identified as strength, strength being the ability to resist the sort of breakage which occurs under strain. It involves such things as the nature of integrative structures, the degree of sense of community,

the extent to which people feel benevolent or malev-
olent toward each other, and so on. The measure of the
strength of the system is the degree to which it can stand
strain but, as the measure of strain is the degree to which
it can overcome strength, it is hard to get independent
measures of these characteristics. We see this, for instance, in the engineering problem of strength of materials. This is ordinarily measured by applying different
degrees of strain to materials and seeing when they
break. This, however, necessitates an independent measure of strain in terms of foot-pounds or something like
that. Otherwise, we would never know whether the
material broke because the strength was too little or the
strain was too great.

In social systems it must be admitted that it is hard
to find independent measures of strength and strain,
though the concepts are clearly meaningful. This leads
to troublesome difficulties in interpretation. A point
of semantics should be clarified here. I use the word
"strength" not in the frequently accepted sense of the
ability to create strain through, for instance, violence but
in terms of the ability to resist strain. These are two very
different meanings of the word. Unfortunately, I find it
a little hard to think of a substitute. It is curious how
ambivalent our vocabulary is in this respect. Even the
word "tough" has two meanings: either being highly
resistant to strain or, in a human sense, capable of im-
posing strain, as in the expression "tough guy." There
may be something deeply significant in this semantic
ambiguity, but it is not my present purpose to inquire
whether there are deep subconscious and psychoanalytic
forces underlying ambiguities in language. This particular ambiguity, however, has created real difficulties in

thought about these problems. In what follows, therefore, I shall use the term strength in its meaning of strain resistance unless I clearly indicate that the other meaning is involved.

There is a further ambiguity in the use of the word "strength" in war-peace systems. The transition from peace to war takes place when the strain on the peace system is too great for its "peace strength." The transition from war to peace takes place when the strain on the war system is too great for its "war strength"— meaning by this again not the capability of any of the parties to wage war but the strength of the total system to sustain war, which usually depends on the willingness of one of the parties to sue for peace. War strength in this sense may perhaps be regarded as the reciprocal of peace strength, for as one rises the other falls. They are not, however, simply the obverse of each other, for the conditions which lead to resistance to the transition from peace to war are in many respects different from those which lead to resistance to the transition from war to peace. For the sake of simplicity in the exposition, however, I am neglecting this difference, as it does not alter the basic pattern of the model.

The strain-strength-break model has wide applicability. If I break a piece of chalk, it is because the strain was too great for the strength of the material. If a bridge or a building collapses, the same model applies. If a marriage breaks down into divorce, the same principle applies: the strain on the relationship was too great for its strength. The same principle would apply to the breakdown of an industrial relationship into a strike, the breakdown of a community into a riot or a civil war, and, likewise, the breakdown of a condition of peace between two countries into a condition of war.

In war-peace systems, of which, of course, the international system is the most prominent, the strain-strength-break model has two levels of application. It can be applied, as we shall see later, to the transitions in the general phases of the system—for instance, from unstable peace into stable peace. It is also useful in explaining the transition process between the special phases, that is, from peace to war and from war to peace in conditions of unstable war or unstable peace.

We can think here in terms of the strain on the key decision makers of the system, those who have the power to declare war or to negotiate an armistice into peace. It is not always easy to identify these people, for there are subtle differences between power and influence, and the decision of one who occupies a position of formal power in the hierarchy, such as a monarch or a prime minister, is always influenced by the communications received from surrounding people and from other sources of information, such as telegrams from diplomats, communications with the press, and so on. Under the condition of peace, we often observe rising tensions and strained behavior on the part of potential opponents which seem threatening. The rising strain is almost always mutual and indeed is self-generating, as an increase in the strain of one party tends to produce behavior which increases the strain of the other, until it rises past some kind of threshold of strength in the system and a fateful decision is made to declare war, to mobilize an army at a frontier, to invade, or to take some other irretrievable step which precipitates similar steps on the part of the other party and the transition from peace into war is effected.

The transition from war into peace has some similarities with the transition from peace into war, but there are also important differences. To go back to the metaphor of the chalk, breaking a piece of chalk is a somewhat different kind of operation from gluing the two pieces together, so it would not be surprising to find certain asymmetries between the peace-war transition and the war-peace transition. There are also similarities in the two transitions from the point of view of the individual powerful decision maker. Here again we could visualize the war-peace pattern as one in which the strain of the war system itself increases and becomes increasingly intolerable, until one party or the other is unwilling to continue the war and sets up communications which lead to a cease-fire, some sort of cessation of hostilities, an armistice, and eventually peace. The initiator of these acts is usually regarded as the loser. If the overtures are accepted, the winner is likely to be in a position to make peace on the winner's terms. Because of the vast misunderstanding of social dynamics on the part of almost all powerful decision makers, it often happens that the loser in a war emerges better off than the victor for the next generation or so. But what matters at the time of the transition from war to peace is that the strain on the decision maker, either on one side or the other, overcomes the strength of the war system and the willingness to continue the war.

From the point of view of the system as a whole, the transition from war into peace also represents an increase in the strength of the system considered as an integrative structure. This may arise simply out of war weariness, the feeling, perhaps unconscious, on one side or the other or both that the war is simply not worth the cost and that both parties would be better off if they came to terms and worked together. Unless this happens, the system will remain in the war phase and will become a system of stable war; this is not unknown in human history.

We can express these changes of phase from war into peace and back again in figure 2, where we show the war-peace cycle. Here we measure the strength of the system horizontally, without bothering at this point to define it too closely, and we measure the strain on the system vertically. Any point in the diagram then represents a particular combination of strength and strain. We then postulate a phase boundary OA which divides the field into a war phase and a peace phase. In the figure we have drawn this boundary starting from the origin, assuming that, with very small strengths, even a very small strain will take the system from peace into war. The boundary does not have to be a straight line, but it seems likely that it will be reasonably linear. The broken line then shows a war-peace cycle. Suppose we start from point B where the system is in peace, with a strength of OH and a strain of HB. We now suppose that the strain rises, due to some interactional dynamic of the system or, even, due to random changes, and that many of the factors that make the strain rise also diminish the strength. The system moves from B to C and we cross the phase boundary into war. At this point there is likely to be a sharp discontinuity; the strain will increase very rapidly under the collapse of taboos, the incidence of atrocities, and the like. The strength of the system will likewise decline to D. As the war proceeds the strain

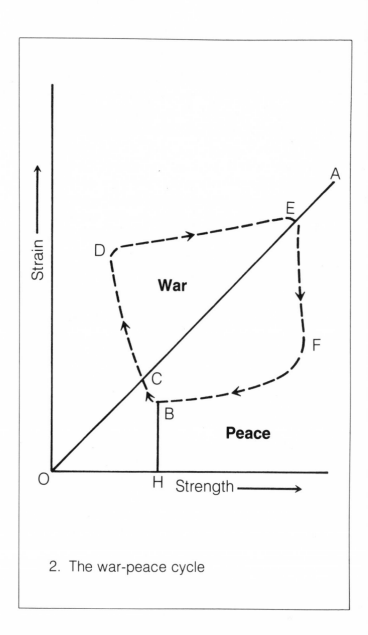

2. The war-peace cycle

on the system may continue to rise, but the underlying peace strength will rise faster as people get tired of the war, as it becomes delegitimated, as the military get discredited, and as the pressures for peace rise. At point E we cross the phase boundary again into peace. Again, there is likely to be a sharp discontinuity, a sudden reduction of strain, perhaps even some increase in strength. As peace continues, however, the strength of the system declines—old hostilities reassert themselves, revanchism appears, there is increasing dissatisfaction with the peace settlement, particularly perhaps on the part of the loser but also on the part of the winner, as winning a war always turns out to be disappointing. So the strength of the system gradually declines to point B, where the whole cycle starts again. The cycle, of course, will never be perfectly repeated.

It is possible for the cycle to move wholly to one side or the other of the phase boundary. This is shown in figure 3. If the strain on the system is very great and the strength is very weak, we get stable war, as in cycle BCDE. We start off, say, at B, a point of fairly low strain, but the strain rises and the strength falls to C. Then there may be some war weariness. But, even if the strain continues to rise, the strength increases somewhat to D. The strain may even fall while the strength increases to E. However, we never pass the boundary into peace. The strength then declines along with the strain, and we get down to B again. In a system of stable peace (shown in cycle B'C'D'E'), starting from B' the strength of the system declines and the strain rises to C'. As the boundary is approached, however, the parties become very much aware of this and are concerned about it and take steps to increase the strength of the system, so that

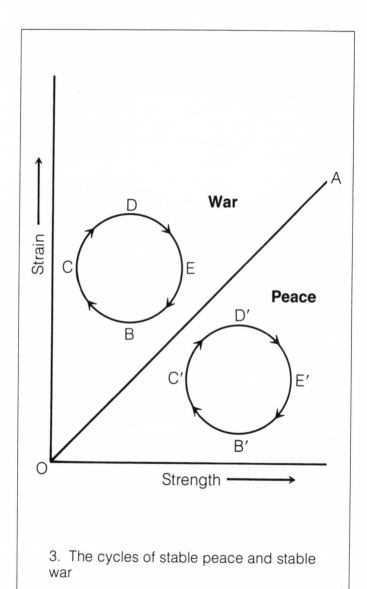

3. The cycles of stable peace and stable war

even though the strain may continue the strength of the system is increased, and it rises to D′. Then the strain diminishes to an increasing strength of E′, the strength diminishes with an increasing strain to B′, and the cycle starts again. As the cycle never actually crosses the phase boundary, there is likely to be less discontinuity. If there is a continued secular increase in the strength of the system, independent of strain—as a result, let us say, of increased communication, increased political union, increased sense of community—the cycle will move in a kind of spiral, as in figure 4, from stable war through unstable war, into unstable peace, into stable peace.

On a somewhat larger scale, the strain-strength-break model may be applied to the transitions of the system at large between the four phases outlined above—stable war, unstable war, unstable peace, and stable peace. The break may not be a dramatic event, it may indeed be quite unperceived at the time by any of the parties, and it may be quite hard to say when the actual transition took place. It does represent, however, a transition from one general system of war-peace relationships to another general system.

We can also represent this model by a phase diagram, as in figure 5. With high strain and low strength we have stable war, with a phase boundary AB between stable war and unstable war. Similarly, with high strength and low strain, we have stable peace, with a phase boundary CD between this and unstable peace. There is a vague boundary between unstable war and unstable peace, EF. If we start from a position of stable war at H, we could reach stable peace at K by a simple diminution of strain without any increase in the strength of the system. We could also start at H and move to

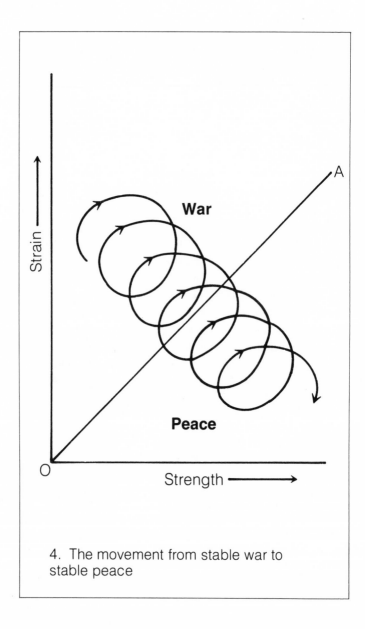

4. The movement from stable war to stable peace

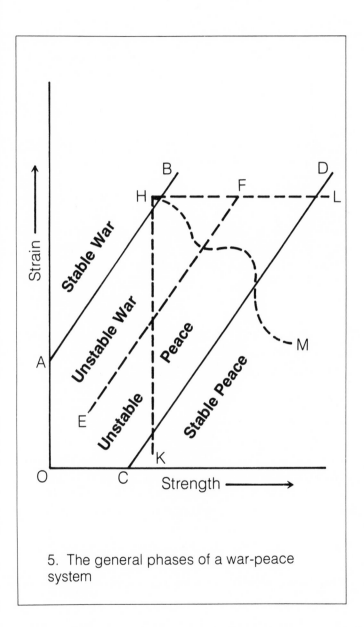

5. The general phases of a war-peace system

stable peace at L by a simple increase in strength, without a diminution of strain. The most likely course would be an irregular path like HM, with strain diminishing as strength increases.

North America in the past two hundred years is an interesting illustration of this type of process. The development of stable peace between the United States and Canada may have something to do with the fact that both were expanding into a large territory and this reduced the strain between them. On the other hand, the increase in the strength of the system of relationship in terms of a political learning process, a development of community, and so on is a factor not to be dismissed. It is clear that from, say, 1776 to sometime after 1812 the general system of relationships between the United States and Great Britain and its colonies such as Canada was under unstable peace. This unstable peace in fact broke down into war in 1812. It did not break down into war in 1844 ("54-40 or fight"), and it did not break down into war during the American Civil War, when the British almost intervened, but this was because the strain on the relationship did not reach the threshold at which it would overcome the strength. The system, however, remained one of unstable peace almost certainly until after the American Civil War, in the sense that the strain might have been too great for the strength of the system and that war between Great Britain and the United States would have had some degree of probability in the first three quarters, shall we say, of the nineteenth century. After the American Civil War, however, this probability declined so much that at some point—it is hard to say exactly when, perhaps between 1875 and

1890—it was so low that we could say that the system had made the transition from unstable peace into stable peace. After that point the probability of war between Britain and the United States did not seriously enter into the military or the political calculations of either country.

The same is probably true of the relationship between the United States and Mexico sometime after 1848, though it is a little hard to say when. During the Mexican Civil War (1910–1919) there was intervention though no formal state of war between the United States and Mexico but, if the strain had been a little greater, it is certainly not impossible that war might have broken out. After 1919, however, the virtual disarmament of the frontier, and indeed the very low level of armament in Mexico, created a situation in which the probability of war, again, was so low that it was virtually not to be taken into account in the international relationship.

We see a similar movement in Scandinavia, beginning perhaps in the eighteenth century, but certainly noticeable after 1815. Sweden's image of itself as a neutral country made the probability of its intervention even in Denmark at the time of the war between Denmark and Germany very low. The peaceful separation of Norway from Sweden in 1905 was something of a landmark in Western history. Again, there was a positive probability that this might have resulted in civil war if the war party in Sweden had been more dominant, but the long tradition of neutrality in Sweden and the relative weakness of the war party, perhaps because this neutrality had been accompanied by very successful economic development in the preceding fifty years, meant that the strain

on the system did not rise to the point where it overcame
the strength. There was no war, and undoubtedly both
parties benefited from the separation.

In Western Europe we have seen a substantial rise in
the strength of the international system since the Second
World War, with the development of the Common
Market. At the moment certainly the probability of war,
shall we say, between France and the Federal Republic
of Germany seems so low that we could claim that we
have made the transition from unstable peace to stable
peace. The relation between the United States and the
Soviet Union is more dubious, but even here one can see
in the movement toward détente a certain movement
toward stable peace. It is still too soon to say that this
has been achieved. In fact, one suspects that it will not
really have been achieved until there is substantial and
effective disarmament, especially of the European frontier. It seems to me that relations between the United
States and the Soviet Union are something like those
between the United States and Britain around, say, 1850.
The probability of war is quite low, but it is not negligible, and a sufficient strain on the system might push
us over the parapet. However, the transition to stable
peace is by no means inconceivable. With a combination
of good luck and good management we should be able
to do it.

Transitions between other phases of the system are
much harder to identify, and perhaps they are not so important as the ultimate transition into stable peace. One
could make a case, for instance, that the situation in the
Middle East ever since 1948 has been one of unstable
war rather than unstable peace—that is, in a sense war
has been regarded as the norm because of the high level

of hostility of the parties involved, and even though there have been quite long intervals of peace these tend to have been used to prepare for the next war. The system has been hovering around the breaking point, in the case of both peace and war, and it is not surprising, therefore, that it has gone over the edge on three or four occasions as a result of some decision maker's finding the strain intolerable and taking the step into war. It has also, however, made the transition from war into peace on an equal number of occasions, as the strain of war became too great and the fear of what might happen if the war continued became greater than the fear of peace. Whether the system is now moving into a phase of unstable peace rather than unstable war is a moot question, though there are distinct signs that this may be happening.

The fact that war-peace systems are really phase systems, whether this involves the immediate transition between war and peace or whether it involves the larger phases of stable or unstable war or peace, means that the discussion of the causes of war is almost universally unsatisfactory. One is tempted to state indeed, with some minor reservations, that the whole concept of the causes of war is useless and that the attempt to find such causes, which occupies a large and unrewarding literature, is as futile as trying to find a cause for the success of a gambling operation. War and peace are part of the vast Shiva's dance of the universe in which everything has multiple causes and multiple effects, in which the attempt to identify the sole cause of anything is doomed to frustration. To go back to the piece of chalk, did it break because the strain was too great or because the strength was too little? In the literal sense, this is an almost meaningless question. The chalk broke because the strain was too great for the strength.

If, however, we are beginning to talk about policy for the future (for instance, decisions which will lead to the chalk's not breaking in the future), the question as to whether it is easier to increase the strength or diminish the strain is certainly not meaningless. I could quite easily take a piece of chalk and not break it, simply by not putting too much strain on it. On the other hand, it is very hard to increase the strength of the chalk. If we make it too strong, it probably won't write on the blackboard. With a steel bar in the middle, it will scratch the blackboard. If we put it in a wooden container, it keeps wearing down and it still won't write on the blackboard. It is obvious that, if we are going to have a policy about not breaking chalk, it will certainly be directed toward reducing strain rather than increasing strength. Similar questions can be asked about any social policy, but it is surprising how infrequently this kind of question is asked. We tend to assume, for instance, that the only way to deal with crime is to increase the police. We believe that this increases the strength of the system and its ability to resist the strain imposed on it by criminals. But we seldom ask whether an increase in police will not itself increase the strain as well as the strength or whether there is anything we can do to diminish the strain in terms of direct intervention in the potential criminal subculture.

It is very important, therefore, to try to trace the dimensions both of strain and of strength in all social relations, especially in the war-peace relationship. This is by no means easy to do. The dimensions are numerous and they are often closely interrelated, so it is hard to tell whether an increase in one may not be offset by a decrease in another. We can theoretically postulate a strain function in which strain is written as a function of a large number of relevant variables. We can similarly postulate a strength function. This does not get us very much farther unless we can identify the variables of the functions and the relations among them. What follows is an extremely tentative listing. A great deal more research needs to go into this field. Each of these sets of variables relevant to strain or strength may be divided into two broad categories. One might be called the structural variables, which describe the general structure and pattern of the system; the other, the dynamic variables, which create an increase or a decrease of strengths and strains. This is a rough division; the two categories will overlap, but it is a way of organizing our thought about the problem.

Looking first, then, at the structural variables of the strain system, we have the images of the past, particularly the memory of past wars, past injustices, and past oppressions. When these are strong, the system has a high structural strain. We see this, for instance, in ancient and traditional hostilities like those between the French and the Germans for the last 150 years, between the Protestants and the Catholics in Ulster, the Greeks and the Turks in Cyprus, the Moslems and the Christians in Lebanon, the Moslems and the Hindus in India —the list, unfortunately, can be multiplied, for there is hardly a single part of the world in which images of the past of this sort are not continually perpetuated. They are all too often reinforced by further outbreaks of hostility and repression, which further reinforce the disastrous images of the past. These images of ancient wrongs are eroded—though painfully slowly—if time goes on without further reinforcement, but continual, periodic reinforcement is all too probable. Whether changes in ideology or in the moral system can assuage these memories and images is an important question, though unfortunately difficult to answer. Could an ideology of forgetting the Alamo and forgetting the hundreds of Alamos in human history take hold? Then the present might be released from its iniquitous enslavement to the past. One cannot be too optimistic about this.

Another important structural variable which reflects strain is the degree of professionalization of conflict, as embodied, for example, in organized armed forces, police forces, the Mafia, competitive missionary movements, unions and employees' associations, and lawyers. There is a great social dilemma here. The existence of strain and the existence of positive probabilities of breakdown into open conflict must inevitably produce professionalization of people whose prime business is to engage in conflict when it occurs. The professional success of these people, however, depends on conflict, and they have a professional interest in maintaining conflict, at least at the level where their services are perceived to be required. Counteracting this, there is a certain professional and political ethic that professional fighters should not themselves promote fights. This ethic is by no means negligible in its impact. One example is the slow growth of civilian control over the military. This, though often precarious, is a meaningful trend in human history and has some modifying influence.

This is not to say that wars are always more likely if the military control a society. Sometimes this is true and sometimes it is not. There is not much evidence that states in which the military are subordinate to a civilian power are much less belligerent and much less likely to engage in war than states which are actually governed by the military. That wars have occasionally been promoted by the military—seeking adventure and justification for their existence—or by the makers of armaments—seeking to expand their trade—is true to some degree, but that this is a major factor in the incidence of war and peace is generally not true. This problem is by no means confined to the war-peace system. It is unfortunately to the economic interest of doctors to promote disease, of dentists to promote tooth decay, of lawyers to promote litigation, and of teachers to promote education, all beyond some optimum point. The impact of professional ethics in these cases, however, is quite noticeable. Doctors in fact promote public health, dentists promote fluoridation, lawyers can be disbarred for promoting litigation under certain circumstances, though I confess I do not know of any example of a teacher who has gotten into trouble for promoting too much education.

Another structural pattern of society which may affect the strain in the war-peace system is the political structure, particularly the way in which powerful roles in the society are filled and organized. As we have seen, decisions about peace and war are usually made within a very small group, somewhere at the apex of the hierarchy of a society. Sometimes these decisions are triggered by decisions which are made much lower down in the hierarchy. The whole problem of the triggering of decisions in the system, indeed, is very interesting. The decision of a terrorist to assassinate an archduke in

Sarajevo in 1914 triggered a whole series of events which led to the First World War. We could argue, of course, that if it had not happened then it might have happened the next year with some other trigger, as the triggering action was all set up. The domino theory of powerful decisions is not wholly unreasonable, but it is extremely hard to tell where the dominoes are and, if one of them fails to fall, this of course stops the whole sequence. It is virtually impossible to predict—or even to study—these failures in events, for it is much easier to know what *did* happen than what did *not*.

Another problem is, what structures are likely to put lunatics in powerful positions? A psychotic personality like Hitler or Amin can create an enormous amount of strain on the international system, apart from any patterns of interest or conflict. We could presumably assess the various processes in different societies by which people rise into powerful roles to see how psychotic personalities would be eliminated from powerful positions. Surely election, as in the United States, is a certain safeguard against psychotic personalities in powerful places because of the extraordinary publicity associated with electoral processes. The United States has elected a number of rascals to the presidency, but it has never to my knowledge elected a madman. Even people as close to being psychotic as Joseph McCarthy eventually go down to defeat because the glare of publicity is apt to reveal their psychotic tendencies before it is too late. In the case of revolutionary situations, however, and political systems that permit coups, and also in the case of hereditary monarchy, the defenses against the rise of psychotic persons to power are weaker. Revolution is a particularly dangerous method of getting people into power from this point of view. Virtually all revolutions have produced psychotic people in positions of power, whether Hitler, Stalin, or Robespierre, and, in light of the catastrophic policies of the Great Leap Forward and the Cultural Revolution, I am not sure I would exempt Chairman Mao. A hereditary monarchy can even produce genetic defects if there is too much inbreeding, like the Hapsburgs, though this seems to have produced incompetence rather than psychosis.

There is a proposition which I have called the dismal theorem of political science—the abilities which lead to the rise to power almost invariably unfit people for exercising it. This is particularly true when the rise to power is a result of revolutionary upheaval. Even in democracies the principle is by no means unknown, though fortunately it is not universal. The principle of checks and balances enshrined in the American Constitution is an attempt to provide safeguards against the abuse of power. As we saw in the case of President Nixon, the system does sometimes work, however clumsily, and it represents a real social invention on the part of the founders of the American republic. The American Revolution indeed seems to be the one great exception to the principle that revolutions throw up people peculiarly unfit to exercise power, for it was not followed by either a Napoleon or a Stalin. Perhaps this was because it was a very small revolution and changed very few of the basic institutions of the society.

Another of the structural characteristics of society which can affect the peace strength of the system is the prevailing ethos, ideology, poetry, history, and educational processes of the society—all of which might be summed up in its "esprit" or spirit. The spirit of a so-

ciety can be either warlike or peaceable, imperial or self-
contained, reactive or placid, aristocratic or bourgeois,
over a wide range of characteristics which do, however,
tend to cluster on the peace strength continuum. How
societies get the spirit they have, however, is a real puz-
zle. There are many historical examples of societies
which have started out very much alike but which have
followed, often it would seem by accident, courses which
have carried them to very different positions. There even
may be a certain cyclical movement between high and
low peace strengths. Thus Sweden changed from a militaristic, imperial society with very low peace strength
under Gustavus Adolphus to a self-contained, peaceable
society even in the eighteenth century. This paid off extremely well in the nineteenth and twentieth centuries,
when Sweden moved from being one of the poorer countries of Europe in 1860 to about the richest country today. Britain and France, after centuries of militarism and
imperialism, moved sharply in the Swedish direction
after 1945. Germany has been remarkably unstable:
devastated by the Thirty Years' War of 1618 to 1648;
relatively peaceable, and the architectural and musical
center of Europe, in the eighteenth and early nineteenth
centuries; imperial and militaristic from 1870 to 1945;
peaceable again from 1945. The dynamics of esprit are
mysterious. Military defeat, for instance, may sometimes
produce a shift away from militarism, as it seems to have
done in Sweden in the seventeenth century; or it may
produce a reinforcement of militarism, as it did in Germany between 1919 and 1945. Often a single charis-
matic leader can set the whole tone of a society. A great
deal more historical and theoretical research needs to go
into this problem.

If we now look at the dynamic processes which can increase or diminish strain, the most dramatic is certainly the arms race. This is a very familiar process and its theory has been well worked out by Lewis Richardson, among others.[1] Nations presumably increase their armaments in times of peace because they feel insecure at the existing level of armaments in light of potential enemies. When one nation increases its armaments, however, its potential enemies find their security diminished, so they tend to increase theirs too. This may lead to a further increase in the first nation, still more increases in the second, and so on in an upward spiral. This process may come to an equilibrium short of war if the parties concerned become unreactive; that is, if a unit increase in the armaments of one country produces a less than unit increase in the armaments of the other.[2] This equilibrium may take place because of increasing strain on the internal system produced by an increase in armaments and the sacrifice this involves for the people of the country in terms of goods and services.

The danger here is that, the richer a society is, the more it can afford to spend on arms and the stronger the tendency, therefore, for the arms race to go on. As it goes on, however, it is likely to increase the strain on the system until it may go over the edge into war. I have shown that, the more parties there are in an arms race, the more stringent are the conditions that would permit an equilibrium and the more likely it is that the arms

1. Lewis F. Richardson, *Arms and Insecurity: A Mathematical Study of the Causes and Origins of War* (Chicago: Quadrangle Books, 1960).
2. Kenneth E. Boulding, "The Parameters of Politics," *University of Illinois Bulletin* 63 (July 15, 1966): 1–21.

race will proceed to war. Whether there is a position of equilibrium or not depends very much on the reactivity coefficients, that is, the amount by which one country will increase its arms compared to a perceived unit increase of the other. The larger the number of countries involved, the smaller this coefficient must be if any equilibrium is to be attained.[3] This proposition underscores the desperate danger of nuclear proliferation, for if a large number of countries have nuclear weapons each, as it were, is at the mercy of any one of the others, and the chances of stability are very slim.

Another dynamic process which has something in common with the arms race might be called repression races. This is particularly characteristic of states with different ideologies, each of which is trying to subvert the other as, for instance, in North and South Korea. Each state finds its fear of the other pushing it into more and more repressive domestic policies, which often defeat themselves by producing internal strain, which in turn produces the external strain in the international relationship. It is a somewhat undecided question as to how far international strain reflects internal strain. The commonsense view would certainly suggest that it does to some degree, and one could probably find cases in which the rulers of nations have gone in for foreign adventures in order to divert attention from their deficiencies at home. Research, however, suggests that this is not necessarily a very general pattern and that it is not a very large element in the strain function,[4] though fur-

3. Ibid.
4. See especially Ted R. Gurr and Vaughn F. Bishop, "Violent Nations, and Others," *Journal of Conflict Resolution* 20 (March

ther work on the nature and effects of internal strain might well reverse this conclusion.

Two dynamic sources of internal strain should be mentioned. One seems more important in short-run movements; this is the sudden worsening in general economic conditions, as in the depression phase of a business cycle or of the political cycles which plague the centrally planned economies. The Great Depression of the 1930s was the greatest of these in recent times, and it unquestionably had something to do with the rise of Hitler in Germany and the slide toward the Second World War. The first collectivization of agriculture in the Soviet Union in the same period, while it produced an even more disastrous worsening of the economy, with the loss of 5 million people and almost half their livestock, did not seem to produce much change in ideology, though it may eventually have produced the Khrushchev reaction into a more peaceable stance. Here again the reaction to adversity is highly unpredictable and may be toward peaceableness or toward militarism.

The second source of internal strain is long-run and is often imperceptible over short periods. This is the relative population growth of segments of society that are perceived as distinct, whether by reasons of race, religion, occupation, class, or any other characteristic. This might be called the "outbreeding" problem. Differential migration of different groups could be regarded as part of the same problem. What role this has played in the history of war and peace is not easy to determine, particularly as the demographic data of the past are so de-

1976): 79–110. See also Jonathan Wilkenfeld, ed., *Conflict Behavior and Linkage Politics* (New York: McKay, 1973).

fective. There are a number of parts of the world today where this phenomenon is not unimportant—Sri Lanka, Guyana, Fiji, and even, in a lesser degree, Britain, the Soviet Union, and the United States. There tends to be a crisis at the tipping point, when a previous minority becomes a majority or, more generally, when the demographic basis of an old dominant group erodes to the point where a new dominant group emerges.

Differential growth, not only of population but of wealth and power, is an important source of strain in the international system. At any one time the international system tends to have a rough pecking order, rather like hens in a barnyard, which is reflected in subtle forms of protocol and behavior. This pecking order reflects a certain ranking of power, that is, pecking power. Pecking power is a function of many things, especially of economic power, as reflected roughly in the total gross national product in constant prices, modified by what I have elsewhere rather unkindly called a coefficient of disagreeability, closely related to the imperialistic or peaceable component of esprit. Disagreeability, however, fluctuates irregularly, as noticed earlier. The gross national product is capable of long periods of growth, stagnation, or decline. The relative dynamics of economic growth, therefore, has a profound effect on pecking orders in the international system and may create periods of cumulative strain. The moment of overtake is particularly dangerous, at which one nation overtakes another either in its GNP or in the pecking-order power ranking. Some wars historically can be tentatively identified as overtake wars. The Napoleonic Wars represent roughly the overtaking of France by Britain as a result of Britain's industrial revolution. The

Franco-Prussian War of 1870 may represent the overtaking of France by Germany. Japan overtook Russia, at
least in East Asia, about the beginning of the twentieth
century. The United States overtook Europe in the First
World War, Japan overtook Europe in the Second
World War, and the United States overtook everybody.
On the other hand, sometimes there is an overtake that
results not in war but in a peaceful change in national
images and national interests. Thus, the United States
overtook Britain about 1870, but this did not result in
war, though the American Civil War came close to it.
Once we come to the degree of maturity that recognizes
that pecking orders are literally for the birds, and that
wars are an absurdly costly method of testing them, this
source of strain may diminish. It is very important to
recognize that the national interest, of which so much
has been made by some writers in this field, is a variable
of the system, not a constant, and that the national interest is what a nation is interested in; it is a property,
indeed, of the national image, which constantly changes.
It may have some objective boundaries in terms of well-
being and survival, but these are usually very wide, and
within these limits the national interest is an essentially
subjective phenomenon.

Another element of strain which might be put either
in the structural factors or in the dynamic factors is the
perceived structure of conflict itself. That there are real
conflicts and that these have some effect on determining
the pattern of wars is so much part of conventional wisdom that it seems almost preposterous to challenge it,
and indeed it is hard to find any conventional wisdom
that does not have some element of truth in it. The
structure of real conflict in society, however, is so com-

plex that there may be very little relation between the intensity of perceived conflict and some kind of objective estimate as to what the real conflicts in society are like.

As noted in chapter 1, we can theoretically divide the human population into three interest groups with respect to any particular policy or event. There are those who are favorably affected, those who are unfavorably affected, and those who are unaffected. It is easy to postulate such a division, however, but it is extraordinarily difficult to do it, and there seems little doubt that the real interest groups in society are very different from those which are perceived. However, only perceived interests, either common or divergent, can affect human behavior. It is not unreasonable to suppose that there is some tendency for the perceived interest to move toward the real interest, but the tendency is often weak because of the difficulty in detecting the sources of either favorable or unfavorable change in one's perceived condition.

Conflicts of economic interest are particularly difficult to identify because of the sheer ecological complexity of the social system. Occupational groups like carpenters or wheat farmers perhaps come closest to an economic interest group, in the sense that a rise in the price of their product will tend to benefit the group at the expense of everybody else in varying proportions. One suspects, therefore, that economic conflict in any real sense is a very weak variable in the strain function, though a perceived conflict may be an important variable. Our perceptions are apt to depend much more on symbolic and ideological perceptions of difference or threat than on any real economic interests. This holds for class conflict as well as for national conflict. There is practically no event which will benefit the working class as a whole and injure the employing class or the capital-ist class. There is practically no event which will benefit all the people of one country and injure all the people of another.

A careful study of imperialism reveals a surprisingly loose connection between human behavior and any kind of real interest. It has become very clear from a number of studies that—in the nineteenth century at least—im-perialism almost always injured the imperial power, or at least most of the people in it, and that the people who benefited from it in the imperial power were very few.[5] Loss of empire has almost always resulted in the im-perial power's getting richer and sometimes in the col-onies' getting richer too. The idea that the riches of im-perial power come from the exploitation of colonies simply does not stand up to any kind of examination.

There are some possible exceptions to this rule of the diffuseness of economic conflict. A cartel, such as the Organization of Petroleum Exporting Countries, can re-distribute income quite sharply toward itself from the purchasers of its product, and this may increase the strain on the international system. Historically indeed there have been wars for the use of resources, of which the long wars of European invaders against the Amer-ican Indians would be an example. The wars which es-tablished the state of Israel might be another example. These wars, however, have always been among markedly unequal groups from the point of view of technology of organization, production, and weaponry. Wars of re-source conquest seem less likely in the modern era,

5. Kenneth E. Boulding and Tapan Mukerjee, eds., *Economic Imperialism* (Ann Arbor: University of Michigan Press, 1972).

though one cannot perhaps wholly rule them out. Certainly some covetous eyes have been laid upon the Arab oil countries with their immense resources and their small populations. So far, however, the perceived dangers of military intervention seem to have created a situation where the strength of the system has been greater than the strain, though at one or two moments we seem to have come perilously close to the phase boundary. Even in the case of the European invasion of North America, it should be noted that there were many occasions in which the purchase of land was cheaper and more successful than conquest.

The strength functions are even more complex than the strain functions. It is quite hard to identify the particular variables which are significant in building up the peace strength of a war-peace system, partly because many of the variables which affect the strain on the system also affect the strength. Again, for instance, memories of the past are important. Like war, peace can become a habit in countries which have been at peace over several generations, such as Canada and the United States, and the habit of peace becomes so strong that even strains on the system are fairly easily handled. This indeed is a certain source for optimism: the longer peace persists the better chance it has of persisting, simply because peace itself increases the strength of the system.

There are also professional specializations which increase the structural strength of the conflict system: mediators and conciliators, for instance, in industrial relations; marriage counselors in family life; and diplomats in the international system. It may be that diplomacy is war continued by peaceful means, but it *is* peaceful, and the long history of the rise of diplomacy may suggest that it plays a role in the achievement of the movement from unstable war into unstable peace and even into stable peace. It is very hard to tell, of course, how much diplomacy is a substitute for war, and there may be times when it exacerbates a system and increases the strain rather than the strength. On the whole, one is inclined to give it good marks in spite of its tendency to corrupt information. Somewhat related to diplomacy is the whole set of structures involving things like royal marriages and the network of integrative relationships among rulers. This certainly did not prevent the First World War in Europe, but it does provide something of a structure and there is evidence, for instance, that it has been important historically.[6]

Another element of the system which can increase strength is the rise of travel and communication, though this may be ambiguous in its effects. Sometimes indeed travel narrows the mind. On the other hand, there does seem to be some relationship between the amount of communication between two countries and their chance of remaining at peace. This is a loose relationship, however, and we should not put too much confidence in it. For instance, as mentioned in chapter 1, there is very little evidence to suggest that a common language is much of a source of strength.

The web of economic interdependence is undoubtedly a significant variable both structurally and dynamically, though it is very complex and it is not always easy to see which way it will go. As we have seen, dependence on imported food may increase the strength of a system. The classical economists certainly thought trade would

6. Bullough and Naroll, *Deterrence in History*.

bring peace simply because it would produce mutual dependency. In this we have been somewhat disappointed. But the effects may still be there. The breaking off of trade and investment relations is one of the costs of war, and one hopes that, the higher the cost of war, the greater the strength of the system. This is indeed a source for modest optimism, as an increase in the cost of war may diminish the willingness to go to war and so indirectly increase the strength of the system, though this may also be offset by an increase in strain.

A worrying problem is whether an increase in the strength of the system might not actually increase the probability of major wars and major catastrophes by preventing a succession of small adjustments. There is somewhat the same problem in flood control, for protecting a floodplain against small floods may encourage people to build on it and hence may make the big flood that cannot be controlled all the more destructive. A system of deterrence may be particularly dangerous in this regard: by increasing the cost of war it may contribute toward short-run stability, as the last thirty years have shown. On the other hand, a system of deterrence must always have within it a positive probability, however small, that it will break down; otherwise it would cease to deter. If the probability of nuclear weapons going off were zero, then obviously they would have no deterrent effect at all. If they are to have a deterrent effect, there must be at least a small positive probability that they will go off. But, however small the probability, if we wait long enough, they will go off. There is a very fundamental proposition here that an event with an annual probability of n is virtually certain to occur sometime within $10/n$ years. At the moment nuclear war looks rather like a hundred-year flood; that is, its annual probability is probably not more than 1 percent. However, the probability of a hundred-year flood happening sometime within any given hundred years is about 63 percent, and its occurrence sometime within a thousand years is 99.995 percent: it becomes a virtual certainty.

The most productive changes to look for with regard to the long-run dynamic of increasing the probability of peace and diminishing that of war are undoubtedly those which both increase the strength of the system and diminish the strain on it. Of these, the movement of national images toward compatibility, particularly with regard to frontiers, will have a high priority. From the point of conflict resolution and getting on in life generally, it is pretty clear that there is an optimum amount of apathy. Children tend to have strong orderings—everything has to be just right or they make a fuss. As we get older we learn to relax our orderings and make them weaker. A lot of different situations suit us about equally well. We put up with things and we stop making a fuss. In the maturation process one suspects that even nations learn to do this. And that, as we come down from the high and dangerous peaks of the heroic, the strains on the system diminish and the strengths increase and the chances of peace improve. Frontiers are a particularly sensitive issue and, the sooner we take these off everybody's agenda, the better will be the chance for peace.

All in all, cautious optimism with regard to peace is permissible. In the last 150 years or so, we have seen the development of islands of stable peace in the international system in the middle of a general matrix of unstable peace, with some islands also of unstable war.

Stable war has become quite rare. Perhaps Vietnam for over thirty years was almost the only clear example, and now that has abated. The payoffs for stable peace in the modern world are very high, and one hopes that this will induce a learning process which will gradually expand the areas of stable peace. There is some turning point in a process like this at which we change from a situation of islands of stable peace in the middle of an ocean of unstable peace to a situation where the islands grow until they join and we have lakes of unstable peace in the middle of a continent of stable peace. We may be closer to this than we think, and we should guard against too much projection from the past. The fact that we have had a world of unstable peace at best for thousands of years does not mean that it is something that has to go on forever. It is possible to have a profound though frequently imperceptible shift in the nature of the system which carries us, as it were, over a kind of watershed into a very different social landscape. I have often compared the peace movement to the labors of Sisyphus—we push the stone uphill and continually it breaks away from us and rolls down again and we have to start all over again. But the hill is not infinite and it has a watershed, and one day the stone will roll over the watershed and we will be chasing it instead of pushing it.

3. The justice of peace

The human race has been engaged in a long, frustrating, but not wholly unsuccessful quest for peace. This quest, however, is haunted by the specter of the just war. We have seen that war and peace are two phases fairly well distinguished in the social system. Behavior which would be utterly taboo in peace is encouraged in war, so it is not surprising that literature abounds with the justification of such behavior. This is an agonizing dilemma. Benjamin Franklin said that "there never was a good war or a bad peace." He also said, "Even peace may be purchased at too high a price." I recall the great peace debates in England in the thirties. The Peace Pledge Union was accused of wanting "peace at any price." The Reverend Dick Sheppard, its founder, responded that he believed in "love at all costs." Without legitimation of war, it would be impossible. Everytime a fatal decision is made to cross the boundary from peace into war, there must be some internal legitimation, some belief that the cause for fighting is just. The only justification for behavior that in itself is monstrously evil is an overriding sense of righteous purpose.

Another source of the legitimacy of war has been the very danger and suffering it imposes on the participants. I have argued that sacrifice itself creates a sense of legitimacy, simply because if we have made great sacrifices for something we cannot admit to ourselves that they have been in vain, for this would be a deep threat to our identity. I call this a sacrifice trap, in which sacrifice demands still more sacrifice.[1] Bygones may be bygones to the rational mind of the economist, but they are not for the person in search of identity. It is precisely the investment of bygones that creates the identity. Just as the blood of the martyrs is the seed of the church, so the blood of the soldiers is the seed of the state. The legitimacy of the soldier is derived not from the fact that he kills for his country but that he dies for his country. It is the names of those who have died for their country, not the body count, that go on the war memorials. Sacrifice creates sacredness, and one of the hidden and subconscious motivations for war is to increase the sacredness of the national state as well as the credibility of its threats, by the sacrifice not only of soldiers but, in modern days, of civilians also.

The change in the technology of international war, however, has greatly eroded its legitimacy. Perhaps the best social indicator is the war song. The First World War produced dramatic war songs. They were almost nonexistent in the Second World War. The Vietnam War produced only antiwar songs. Part of this arises from mechanization, as it removes the wielders of the

1. Kenneth E. Boulding, *The Economy of Love and Fear: A Preface to Grants Economics* (Belmont, Calif.: Wadsworth, 1973).

weapons from their victims. In the days of the sword and hand-to-hand combat, the killer had a high chance of being killed; this in a sense legitimated fighting behavior on both sides. In this day of Dresden, Hiroshima, and Vietnam, there is total divorce of the bomber from the victims. We cannot ignore also the divorce of the generals, politicians, and decision makers from their victims. There is an erosion of the whole structure of legitimacy of the enterprise of war.

The failure of the United States in Vietnam is striking testimony to the overwhelming importance of legitimacy. In Korea, the United States had at least a shred of legitimacy provided by the United Nations. In Vietnam, it had none, even though the presence of the United States in Vietnam was perhaps inspired more by moral considerations and a desire to preserve the free society than by any consideration of economic gains, which were negligible, indeed negative. Nevertheless, the methods used completely destroyed the legitimacy of the objective. The Communists, in spite of representing an ideology which I believe to be a totally inadequate guide to human betterment, also represented the homeland against the invaders, and they were able to evoke an enormous legitimacy which all the wealth and destructive power of the United States could not overcome. Because we lost the sense of our own legitimacy, the United States was prevented from exercising its potential military power. The Vietnam War never absorbed more than 3 percent of the GNP and was a superb example that you cannot use weapons which you cannot legitimate, even if you have them.

Indeed, the delegitimation of international war has almost certainly diminished the probability of small

wars, but it still means that total war has a small probability which reaches virtual necessity over a long enough
period of time. The legitimacy of internal war, however,
has not been threatened so much by the new weaponry,
as internal war continues to be on a hand-to-hand, guerrilla warfare basis. Therefore, for revolutionary ends or
even for the transfer of power from one internal group
to another, the just war doctrine is still very strong.
Hardly any of us today would declare that a nuclear
holocaust is a just war, and in international war the concept has become increasingly rejected. But there is still,
around the world, internal war: Belfast, Cyprus, Rho-
desia, Uganda, and a large number of other places. Even
in the United States politically motivated bombings and
assassinations are by no means unknown, though they
are small enough in scale so they rarely affect the lives of
ordinary citizens. Even around the world, automobiles
and stepladders are more dangerous to human life than
are guerrilla fighters. Nevertheless, a breakdown of societies into internal war may be more of a danger in the
near future than international war. In Africa, for instance, there was little that could be called an international war outside of Egypt in the last twenty-five years,
until the Ethiopia-Somalia war of 1977, but Biafra,
Burundi, Uganda, the Sudan, Angola, Mozambique, and
many others are all examples of internal war. The experience of the American Civil War and the Mexican
Civil War of 1910 to 1919 suggests that sophisticated
societies are by no means immune to going over these
internal cliffs.

The perceptions of justice and injustice clearly form
an important aspect of both strain and strength in a war-
peace system. A system of peace which is perceived by

increasing numbers of its participants to have elements of injustice will be subject to increasing strain. The strength of the system may depend on a number of rather contradictory characteristics. If the dominant party of a system is self-confident, high in its morale, full of a sense of its own legitimacy, and willing to make and carry out threats, the system may be fairly stable even under a strong sense of injustice. There may be some mixture of threats, legitimacy, and payoffs here which may be unstable, and a small shift may then cause the whole structure to crumble. Sometimes this crumbling takes place very rapidly, as in Russia in 1917 or France in 1789.

The strength of the system may be enhanced by symbols of legitimacy: crowns, scepters, robes, processions, trumpets, dress uniforms, coronations, rituals, and the like. The legitimacy of symbols may erode, however, and become worthless if the strain on the system is too great. Similarly, terror, the absence of taboos on torture and murder, may for a time make people unwilling to challenge the system and may even give it a kind of perverse strength. But these things increase the strain on the system and deepen resentment that is passed on from generation to generation. The sense of injustice ultimately erodes the whole legitimacy of the system and it collapses. Political power that is not based on a profound underlying consent contains the seeds of its own eventual destruction. We cannot fool all of the people all the time, but perhaps we can fool a distressingly large number of them for a distressingly long time.

It is very important to inquire, therefore, what characteristics of a social system create a sense of injustice, which is almost the same thing as a denial of legitimacy.

The psychological nature and the history of each individual are crucial in determining the difference in feelings of injustice from one individual to another. On the other hand, these feelings are not arbitrary or wholly random, and there are some configurations in the outside world which are more likely to be perceived as unjust than others. We can postulate a justice function: $J = f$ [the relevant universe]. In other words, J can be defined as the most probable perception of the justice or injustice of the relevant universe as perceived. The function is easier to define for low levels of J. We perceive injustice much more readily than we perceive justice, just as we perceive the absence of breathable air much more readily than we perceive its presence, which we take for granted. We cannot define any measure of J in terms of social indicators, though most people with some knowledge of the world would be able to give a very rough and uncertain ordering of different societies on the scale of justice. This ordering might differ from place to place, and it would differ of course with people's ideology. People have a certain tendency to value their own society highly. Most Americans regard the Soviet Union as a grossly unjust society, and most citizens of the Soviet Union return the compliment. No concept of fine tuning is possible. Most people would agree that Uganda is a highly unjust society today, but they would be hard put to say whether Canada is a more just society than the United States.

It is very important to inquire into the variables that are regarded as relevant to the perceptions of the level of justice in a society. There is a place here for empirical research. John Rawls argued at great length and with considerable persuasiveness that a sense of fairness may be the major value in the justice function,[2] though I am not sure this does very much more than rename the concept. Rawls does suggest a very ingenious intellectual experiment as an aid to evaluating subjectively the justice of different societies. He asks us to imagine which society we would prefer to be born into if we did not know whom we were going to be. In the United States we might find ourselves being a sharecropper or a Rockefeller; in the Soviet Union we might find ourselves a prisoner in a slave labor camp or a member of the Politburo. The trouble with ferreting out this sort of information is that most people would probably vote for their own societies because they are more familiar. We tend to prefer the devil we know to the devil we do not, but there might be exceptions to this.

Any attempt to identify the variables of the justice function will conclude that equity is one of the components. This in itself is a complex concept with a number of definitions. Perhaps the most important definition would be equal treatment for equal cases. In terms of the law this means that the same crimes should get the same sentences, that people having the same responsibilities should pay the same taxes, that there should be no arbitrary discrimination in jobs or promotion because of characteristics which are irrelevant to the situation. Just what is irrelevant of course may be a tricky question. The movement against racial, sexual, and religious discrimination is clearly motivated by a widespread feeling that the arbitrary exclusion of certain groups from some of the benefits of society cannot be justified. Dis-

2. John Rawls, *A Theory of Justice* (Cambridge, Mass.: Belknap Press, 1971).

crimination oddly enough represents the failure to discriminate, the failure to treat like cases alike and unlike cases unlike, which is a violation of the fundamental principle of equity.

A further pursuit of the principle of equity suggests the further principle of equality of opportunity. This is a very intricate problem, simply because it raises the whole question of inheritance and the right of the family as against the larger community and the rights of property owners in general. Inequality of opportunity arises simply because people are born into different families. A baby born into a rich family, with well-educated and well-financed parents, is likely to have a better chance to develop her or his full potential than a baby born into a family on the edge of a shantytown. Most of the wealthier societies seem to attempt to offset the impact of family inheritance by providing a social inheritance in the shape of free public education, "headstart" programs, aid to dependent children, and so on, but in no country do these public programs more than offset to a small degree the enormous inequality of opportunity that arises from the differences in the status of each family. This is just as true in socialist countries as it is in the free market world. Children born into well-placed families will have much better chances of rising to a prominent place in all societies than children born of peasants, dissidents and sectarians. On the other hand, virtually all societies are reluctant to abandon the family as an instrument of transmission both of nutritional and genetic structure and of social knowledge and skill. We have here a clear example of the conflict of equity with other values, and there has to be some kind of a tradeoff. One of the principles of normative science is that no particular values are absolute, and the tradeoff problem is universal.

A principle which is not to be confused with the principle of equality of opportunity might be called the principle of full realization of potential. Every baby is born into the world with a certain genetic potential for growth, knowledge, skill, love, happiness, and so on. For the vast majority of babies, perhaps indeed for all, this potential is never fully realized because of the limitations of poverty, lack of skill of the parents, unfriendly environments, poor education, restriction of information, and so on. Where there is a strong sense of the nonrealization of human potential because of the environment of the person, there is a sense of injustice or at least dissatisfaction. The realization of human potential, however, may be much more a function of the average wealth and status of the society than it is of any internal distribution. A society may be egalitarian in the sense that every baby born into it has about the same set of opportunities, and yet these opportunities might be highly restricted by the general poverty or cultural pathologies of the society. The overall level of riches, competence, skill, and productivity of the society is an important element in the justice function. This is something beyond equity, which is concerned primarily with distribution.

We must be careful, however, of the conventional measures of the overall level of development in society, such as the per capita GNP. The human being has great potential for evil and pathology as well as for goodness and health. There has to be a critique of the kind of potential which is realized. The society with a high GNP per capita may be full of alienated, strife-ridden, miserable people, and the society that is much poorer as measured by income may produce healthier, more interesting, more fulfilled persons. Yet there is at least a rough relationship between riches and the capacity to fulfill the potential, even though the potential may be misused.

Attempts have been made to define equity in terms of envy.[3] This, again, is very tricky. Envy, like all the deadly sins, tends to have a nonlinear, somewhat parabolic relation with goodness. A little envy may be a spur to achievement, but envy can also become a corrosive and utterly destructive emotion, producing neurosis and internal decay. The demand for equality which is made solely on envy does not strike me as very satisfactory as the foundation for a good society. The radicalism which arises from hatred and envy of the rich has very different results from that which arises from compassion for the poor. Another source of frustration in the demand for justice is what I have called the illusion of the pie. This is a metaphor beloved by economists—that there is a static pie of goodies which is divided among the members of the society, presumably by a rather skillful wielding of knives. In this case the only way to help the poor would be to take away from the rich. Reality is much more complex. There is no single pie, but there is a vast pattern of little tarts, each growing or declining at its own rate. The growing ones get richer; the declining and stationary ones get poorer. Some may stabilize at a good level; others may stabilize at a level of misery. This is not to say that greater equality cannot be

3. H. R. Varian, "Distributive Justice, Welfare Economics, and the Theory of Fairness," *Philosophy and Public Affairs* 4 (1975): 223–237.

achieved by redistribution—there is some spooning from one tart to another—but it is difficult, and it is easy to destroy more than we distribute.

Equality in an absolute sense would be advocated by nobody. On the other hand, it is very clear that there are degrees of inequality in a society which threaten its legitimacy and stability. Again, we can use the Rawls experiment to ask, "Would you rather live in a society in which everyone was equally poor or a society in which some people were as poor as in the first one but others were rich?" Most people would opt for the latter. They prefer some chance of being rich to no chance of being rich. But, on the other hand, suppose we had to choose between a society in which some people were desperately and miserably poor and others were excessively rich (I think most people would define excessively rich as being about twice as rich as they are themselves) and a society in which there was a floor of poverty, so nobody was allowed to fall into destitution even though others might be rich. Then we would almost certainly vote for the second. We would rather have a society where there was no chance of being desperately poor than one in which there was a chance of being desperately poor even though there was also a chance of being filthy rich. What seems to emerge from this discussion is that a moderately unequal society, where there is a floor below which nobody falls, seems to get high marks and should be able to establish a substantial legitimacy and internal stability.

Another set of variables, frequently relevant to perceptions of justice, might be called the oppression-liberation scale. Oppression is perceived when one person or group of persons is seen as becoming better off at the expense of another, dominated group. Domination and submission are perceived as important variables. There is something of a dilemma here as legitimated domination, or legitimated subordination, is essential to any large-scale, hierarchical organization, and how this is legitimated is very important in explaining the dynamics of society. For instance, this legitimation partially explains the success of the European settlers in America in displacing the Indian population. As a matter of fact, the Europeans brought with them a "habit of subordination," as Adam Smith called it, which enabled them to form large organizations.[4] The fierce independence of the indigenous inhabitants prevented them from forming organizations much larger than the family or tribe, so they could seldom offer a united resistance.

My own view is that oppression undoubtedly exists as a secondary cause of human misery but that all the liberation of the world will only go a small way toward solving human problems or resolving the dynamics of the human condition. Nevertheless, the rhetoric has a powerful appeal. It is comforting to think that everything that is wrong with you is somebody else's fault. I grew up myself in a tradition which believed that if something was wrong with you it was probably your fault, at least as a first approximation, and that the view that it was somebody else's fault was a second approximation. It seems to me that on the whole this tradition was psychologically healthy and much more likely to lead to human betterment than the reverse view. Nevertheless, there are important cases of oppression as a

4. Smith, *The Wealth of Nations*, p. 532.

source of human misery—as we see it in dictators around the world; as we saw it in slavery; in serfdom both feudal and communist; and in tyrannies of all kinds, from that of a spouse or a parent to that of a political tyrant. How one deals with this is a question by no means easy to answer, for liberation all too often creates new oppressors. I am more inclined myself to rely on the slow ecological processes that gradually erode the legitimacy and the sources of tyrannical power.

A final element in the justice function is alienation, a term popularized by the Marxists. In their writings the word tends to take on the flavor of the seven deadly sins. Certainly the Marxist concept that alienation arose when somehow the workers lost the product of their labor in the great sewer of exchange has always reminded me a little bit of the psychoanalytic theory that our troubles are due to the fact that our first product was flushed down the toilet. Nevertheless, the concept is important for the light it throws on that removal of taboos which is the prime source of violence. At all times, one suspects, a large majority of people have not been particularly alienated from their own societies and have accepted their life and their environment as pretty much the order of nature. What rumblings of discontent they may have felt have been overlaid by the sheer urgent necessity of making a living and living a life. However, the minority that has felt alienated has been an important source of social change, though it would be a great mistake to think that all such change arises from alienation. I am inclined to think that the largest social changes—the rise of knowledge and skill, the development of science and the arts, and the perpetual kaleidoscope of fashion—are brought about by people who are not alienated from society but who work quietly and unspectacularly within it. It is possible indeed to criticize a society and still not be alienated from it, that is, still feel a part of it. To be alienated is to feel like a foreigner. Large numbers of people get into groups and circumstances and subcultures in which this feeling may arise, and there are certainly some situations where we feel more at home than we do in others. Alienation is a sentiment so unpleasant and so discouraging that most people transform it at least into a grumbling acceptance. One could say certainly that the second-class citizen is more alienated than the first-class and that alienation is a matter of degree, but even a second-class citizen's self-perception is that of a citizen of sorts.

Nevertheless, alienation is an important source of violence. We see this indeed in international war, which is only possible because the enemy is defined as a foreigner and not as a member of the society. Each party in international war is alien to the other, and it is only when this kind of alienation increases to the point where it goes over the normal taboo barrier into violence that war can occur. In internal war, likewise, alienation is of great importance. The Irish Republican Army people who plant bombs which kill the innocent could only do so if they were deeply alienated not only from their own society but in a sense from all society. If they ever thought of their victims as real people, one doubts whether they could bring themselves to these acts. Fortunately, in most human beings alienation rarely rises to this level.

Unfortunately we know very little about the sources of alienation in particular individuals. This is partly because extreme alienation is a rare phenomenon and

hence is difficult to study. It is not caught by sample surveys. Anthropologists rarely apply the methods of par-
ticipant observation to guerrilla groups. Extreme alienation is clearly the result partly of particular and peculiar
experiences of the individuals concerned in terms of
childhood trauma, rejection by people whom they visualize as representatives of the society, and so on. It may
also, however, be a function of the nature and structure
of the society itself. It is at least a reasonable hypothesis
that heterogeneous societies, particularly those in which
certain groups visualize themselves as being in disadvantaged situations, are unusually likely to produce alienation. Groups which perceive themselves to be disadvantaged may not necessarily be minorities; for instance,
women are in a minority nowhere yet may legitimately
feel disadvantaged. Societies which are homogeneous in
culture, mobile with regard to class, and tolerant with
regard to diversity, like Sweden and Japan, are perhaps
the least likely to produce alienation. Heterogeneous,
stratified, rigid, and intolerant societies are more likely
to produce it.

The problem of justice, complex and difficult as it is,
is part of a larger problem of human betterment. Human
betterment is not easy to define and still harder to agree
upon, but it is nevertheless meaningful. We do in fact
evaluate the state of the world as moving either from
better to worse or from worse to better. We do perceive
in the course of the history of the planet that the process
of evolution seems to have a time's arrow toward increasing complexity and toward growth of control or
intelligence, something of which human beings have
more, an amoeba has less, and a crystal still less. In the
evolutionary process something seems to be getting big-

ger. But getting bigger is not necessarily getting better. Betterment implies evaluation by humans of the state of the world around them, including themselves and their artifacts. This state changes all the time according to the overall dynamics of the system, and these changes are constantly being evaluated. Most people only evaluate themselves and their immediate environment. If today they are in good health, have a pleasant material environment, are well fed, secure in their family, and happy in their work, the present is obviously going to be evaluated highly. If tomorrow they get sick, lose their job, are divorced by their spouse, lose a loved one by death, or get demoted, they are going to visualize this situation as worse. We usually do not put numbers to these evaluations—only economists have the nerve to do that. But we do have a fairly strong sense of the direction of the value change, that is, whether things are getting better or getting worse, and we have a certain sense of how much better or worse things are getting.

People differ a good deal in the extent of the environment that they evaluate. There are people who have no hesitation about evaluating the whole state of the world, from the blue whale to the CIA. Some confine themselves to the state of their country or their neighborhood or their family or their own state of mind and body. The more powerful a person, the more likely is she or he to evaluate large environments. In these days of rapid communications and mass media, even people in remote places and in conditions of severe poverty are likely to have a sense that they are part of a much larger environment about which they have some evaluations. Almost everybody nowadays hears some news, and the news may make us feel better or worse about the world—though news should not be relied upon too much, as it tends to be biased toward reporting the worst, this being more concentrated, spectacular, and interesting than most of the good things that happen. It is a somewhat consoling thought indeed that, if values come from scarcity, the fact that the news reflects catastrophes, disasters, accidents, wars, and disturbances in a much larger proportion to other events suggests at any rate that these things are relatively scarce and infrequent and that the good things are not reported simply because they are common and dull. When a newspaper reports only good news, that is the time to get really worried, for this will suggest that the bad news is too commonplace to be reported.

The state of the world is so complex that we try to reduce it to metaphors, indicators, and numbers. One of the great problems in the assessment of the state of the world is that our own personal experience is a very small and biased sample of it. Hence, leaping to conclusions about the state of the world from this personal experience is likely to lead us into serious error. It is indeed one of the main functions of the social sciences to provide a well-sampled description of the state of the world, abstracted enough to be comprehensible without doing too much violation to reality. This is a difficult task and we do not do it very well. Nevertheless, we have made some progress—the development of things like national income statistics and social indicators in the last fifty years, for instance, has had a very profound effect on our image of the world and on expanding this beyond our own personal experience. We must recognize, however, that any abstract and quantitative image of the world is bound to be a very imperfect representation of reality. If numbers like the GNP or other social indicators are taken too literally, they may impair the reality of our image of the world. If they are used wisely and with discrimination, however, they can give us a much more accurate picture of the world than could ever be described from our own personal experience and the news.

We must always remember that our image of the world is not an evaluation of it. A rise in the GNP, for instance, does not necessarily mean things are better; it may only mean that some things are bigger. If these bigger things include a large war industry as well as economic activity to remedy the damages of pollution, a rise in the GNP can be very misleading. Nevertheless, it is not uninformative, and there would be widespread agreement that up to a certain point a rise in the average level of real income, for instance, is for the better. There can always be exceptions to this, especially in individual cases. If, however, an increase in the GNP per capita is accompanied by a change in the distribution of income which is perceived as for the worse, this may offset the increase in the GNP per capita in the overall evaluation. It is quite common, for instance, for an increase in the GNP per capita to be accompanied by an actual worsening in the state of the poorest section of a society. It would not be illogical to define this as a move for the worse, in spite of the fact that 75 percent of the people are better off. Similarly, if the increase in the GNP per capita is accompanied by increased repression, political dictatorships, suppression of minorities, or lack of individuality in the arts and the sciences, as has frequently been the case, we might well make a negative evaluation of the overall change.

We can postulate a goodness function, $G = f$ [the relevant universe], very much like the justice function; on the right-hand side indeed J will be one of the variables. We all evaluate G, the total goodness of the state of "our" world, goodness being defined as what goes up when things get better and what goes down when things get worse. We do this by first describing the state of the world, then assigning goodness weights—something like what economists call shadow prices—to all the different descriptions. These goodness weights will be positive for things that are thought of as good, negative for things thought of as bad. Suppose now that A goes up and B goes down. The overall impact of this on our estimates of goodness depends on the weights which are given to A and to B. Goodness will go up if the sum of the positive evaluations exceeds the sum of the negative ones.

It may be objected that we do not perform these overall evaluations by simple addition, and there is something in the criticism, especially as a change in the quantities of the different elements of the state of the world will change their goodness rates. There is an extension of the economic principle of diminishing marginal utility which says that, the more of anything there is, the less likely an increase of it will give an increase in goodness. There is also the famous principle of the Aristotelian mean, that every virtue becomes a vice if there is too much of it. The goodness weight will be high for small quantities of anything but will decline and eventually become negative as the quantity increases.

There are people who hold, in effect, that certain goodness weights are infinite. As a matter of fact, Rawls comes perilously close to this in arguing for an absolute value for a rise in the welfare of the worst off. The economist, however, shies away from any infinite values and always insists there are likely to be some tradeoffs. There can be too much justice as well as too much freedom, or too much equality, or even too little alienation, in relation to the alternatives that are sacrificed.

A serious problem arises because each individual may have a different evaluation of the state of the world and of the goodness weights which are put on various items. This raises the whole political problem of social organization and coordination. It is much too large to be fully explored here. There are, however, three large processes in social life by which these coordinations of different values and different people are accomplished, at least roughly. I am tempted to call these the three P's: prices, policemen, and preachments. The economist points out that the different preferences of individuals are coordinated through the market and the system of relative prices in exchange. There are propositions to the effect that free exchange and competitive markets produce a situation in which everybody is better off, at least in their own estimation at the time. There are some legitimate questions about these theorems, but they tend to take the form of modifications rather than of outright denials, and the usefulness of exchange and the price structure in coordinating the different evaluations of different individuals without serious conflict suggests that the exchange system is a very valuable social instrument.

Another instrument of coordination is through policemen, that is, the coercive apparatus of the state and its subordinate units. The law involves mainly a body of prohibitions, that is, taboos, with attendant sanctions. Insofar as this creates a tax system, we also get a public grants economy which is capable of constructing organizations and affecting human behavior through rewards —for instance, we hire people to do a job, paying them with government money. The law is a vast accretion— including custom and common law, judicial precedent and legislation—which represents, as it were, the accumulated decisions of the past in some way publicly legitimated. The current activity of legislative bodies, and also to some extent judicial bodies, reflects an apparatus of limited consensus, consensus at least in the sense that the acts of legislators do not produce alienation to the point of organized disobedience and revolt. We may think of political development as a process by which society evolves institutions and political culture which permit the orderly expression and change of this consensus, so that individuals in powerful roles can be replaced in an orderly fashion and the society moves in a constant and orderly way toward a legal system which at least does not violate consensus, even though it may leave a good deal of latitude.

Preachments I use as a metaphor for moral and ethical communications of all kinds, from the lifted eyebrow and the slight edge in the tone of voice which are responses to a breach of etiquette to the thunders of the demagogues, the suggestions of the psychoanalysts, and the legal drama of the Naderites. It seems to be easy for intellectuals to underestimate the volume and significance of ethical criticism, but it has a profound effect on the learning of evaluations. All groups consisting of persons in strong interaction tend to produce a common ethos which checks nonconformity. At a somewhat higher level we have the interactions of groups, but this follows much the same kind of principles. The language

and ethos of almost any group within the United States
will differ quite noticeably from those of similar groups
within the Soviet Union. A national, and even a world,
society creates pressures to conformity among groups.

Another question is the role of the war-peace system,
whether international, internal, or even interpersonal, in
the long evolutionary process toward justice and human
betterment. Simply by taking a sample of the historical
record, one can certainly find wide differences in the
evaluations of the role of war and peace in human betterment. At one extreme we will find those who see in
peace a state of society which will almost inevitably lead
to moral deterioration, debilitating luxury, the decay of
the will, a decline of morale, a process that can only be
cured by the shock treatment of occasional war. These
people see in war something which is cleansing and
purifying by the sacrifices it entails and even the poverty
it produces.

At the other end of the scale—and I must confess this
is where I stand—are those who see war as an outrageous
violation of the human community, in which the military
virtues of courage and self-sacrifice, real as they are, are
merely the reflected colors on the surface of a vast pool
of unspeakable filth and human misery. Peace, on the
other hand, is seen as the normal and proper state of
humanity, pushing the evolutionary process toward the
fulfillment of the biological potential of the human race
in terms of cultural artifacts and activities, unhampered
by pathological threats and destructiveness. The change
in the technology of war has certainly moved large
numbers of people toward the latter view. The injustice
that war perpetrates on its victims is so monstrous that

it far overshadows all the injustice of peace. War destroys equity, for equals are treated grossly unequally, and it has historically been one of the prime sources of inequality, which is to a large extent due to the inheritances of past conquests.

Some nagging questions remain. There is, for instance, the question of the institutions of defense against unwanted change. All change is not for the better, and the problem of defense against unwanted change is a very legitimate one. On the other hand, almost without exception, institutions for defense seem to turn out to be pathological or, at least, have a very easy potentiality of becoming pathological. Even in the human body, defense by antibodies can cause a lot of trouble, and it may well be that some cancers and other forms of breakdown reflect a pathology of the defensive system of the body against organisms that invade it. At the psychological level, defense mechanisms have a bad name. Aggression unfortunately seems to be much more psychologically healthy than defensiveness, even though it causes defensiveness in others. The resolution of this paradox seems to be the development of a positive identity capable of compassionate self-expression and non-pathological defense. In the international system, defense is a deep social pathology that, even in peacetime, gobbles up some 6 to 10 percent of the total product which is desperately needed for other things. The war industry breeds itself in a monstrous symbiosis. The armed forces of two opposed countries are the principal supporters of each other, and their victims are their own civilians. It is, however, a system that is highly intractable. The general problem of a creative organization of defense may go down as the most dangerous unsolved problem of the human race.

Finally, I would raise a question that is surprisingly seldom raised: how important, quantitatively, is the war-peace system in the overall evolution and betterment of the human race? My own answer is that it is sometimes important, but it is far less important than most people, especially most historians and politicians, think. We can put the question in the form, "How often does it really matter who wins a fight?" To the participants it often matters very much—one wins and one loses—but even here the ultimate consequences are by no means clear. Indeed, in terms of economic development in the twentieth century, it has been the losers in war who have been the principal gainers and the winners who have been the losers; Japan and Germany are prize examples. Nevertheless, there have been cases in which the loss of a war destroyed a ruling class or even eliminated a culture, though these cases are surprisingly rare. The Neanderthals perhaps? Carthage? The Aztecs? Mohenjo-Daro? There are not many clear cases. If the great battles of world history had gone the other way, would the history of the human race have been very different? I think not, on the whole, though of course in detail it would have been.

I am convinced it is in the field of what I have called nonconflict—working, producing, buying and selling, learning, thinking, worshiping, loving, procreating— that the mainstream of the human race goes on. This has been true throughout all of biological evolution, where fighting is very rare and relatively insignificant. This does not rule out the possibility that sometimes it does matter who wins a fight. This may happen through what might be called evolutionary watersheds, where a fight may determine the kind of evolutionary potential that will guide the course of the next period. All watersheds, however, eventually end up in the ocean, and we really do not know what matters in the long run.

4. Policy for peace

Where peace has prospered and a social system has
moved toward stable peace, it has usually been the result
of a somewhat accidental dynamic of the system and
has seldom—indeed I think we could safely say never—
been the result of a carefully planned, long-range policy. Nevertheless, we do perceive subsystems in the
history of the planet in which a movement toward
stable peace has taken place and stable peace has been
achieved. In the nineteenth century, it was achieved in
North America and Scandinavia, and there are other
somewhat less secure examples from earlier history. We
see the same phenomenon in internal relations. There
has been, however haltingly, a movement from societies
with bloody internal violence, like the Scotland of *Macbeth* or the France of the St. Bartholomew massacre, to
societies in which the level of internal violence is low
and the society is not threatened by it. According to
Boulding's first law—that anything that exists is possible—benign dynamic processes of this sort must be
possible, and if they are possible they may be fostered
and accelerated by policy; that is, deliberate decisions

may be designed with a conscious, large-scale process of society in view. The movements from bad to worse instead of from bad to better, as we saw in Hitler's Germany, Stalin's Russia, or Amin's Uganda, should give us no cause for despair but, rather, the hope that by a learning process and some deliberate policies we can increase the probability of benign movements and diminish the probability of malign ones.

Perhaps up to the twentieth century there has never been any real necessity for a policy for peace. War has been evil. It has set things back in many places. It has created a large amount of unnecessary human suffering. But it has not been fatal to the ongoing evolution of the human race. We can see a certain parallel perhaps in the matter of the environment. Up to the twentieth century, pollution and environmental disruption and so on were essentially local matters which never threatened the human race as a whole. With the development, however, of a world population of 4 billion that threatens to rise to 8 or even 12 billion before its increase can be halted, and with the increased output of commodities with the accompanying increased output of discommodities, it is quite clear that the human race has to develop some kind of policy for living on the planet and not destroying its own niche.

The situation in the twentieth century is unprecedented in a great many ways. The lessons of history have to be learned very carefully. They teach us a good deal about subsystems but not very much about the earth as a total system, which is what it is becoming. The danger of a total earth system is very great. As long as the earth is divided into a large number of isolated subsystems, as it was before the modern era, a catastrophe could happen in one subsystem without the rest of the world even knowing about it, like the great catastrophe that destroyed the Maya Empire. If the earth becomes a single system, however, everything may go wrong with it if anything goes wrong with it. Catastrophes can easily be afforded in an earth of isolated and diverse systems, simply because they are most unlikely to happen everywhere at once, and the areas that have not suffered can repopulate and restore those that have, but a catastrophe which engulfed the whole earth might be fatal. The probability of such a catastrophe may be very small but, in light of constant technological advances in the means of destruction, we cannot be sure that there will not be a doomsday machine.

When the probability of catastrophe is small, however, we tend to evaluate it in practice as zero. This is why people take airplanes, live on floodplains, on the slopes of volcanoes, on earthquake faults, and in a system of nuclear deterrence. Nuclear deterrence must have a positive probability of failure, no matter how small. If the probability of nuclear weapons going off were zero, that would be equivalent to not having them at all and, if they exist, there must be some probability that they will go off. In this country psychologically we believe that probability to be zero, just as the people in the Big Thompson Canyon behaved as if the probability of a hundred-year flood were zero. If we really believed that the probability of nuclear war were large enough to affect our behavior, we would go in for massive civil defense, and that would drastically increase the probability of nuclear war itself. In a rather similar way flood control projects often increase the probability of major catastrophe, simply because they encourage people to build on a floodplain.

Policy is a lot of different things, and there is no single concept that encompasses it. It means first a strategy of decision, that is, a decision now which sets up a rule for making decisions in the future. Shaving in the morning is a decision. Sometimes if I am staying at home and not seeing anybody I decide not to shave. Being clean-shaven, however, is a policy, and growing a beard is another policy which severely limits the decision which is made every morning. If my policy is to be clean-shaven, I will normally shave; if it is to grow a beard, I will not. Even in this case some kind of image of a system of the world is involved—for instance, that of the tendency of hair on the face to grow. Policy also may involve the setting up of organizations to do things and to make decisions. Marriage is a policy which involves setting up an organization of the family. Government policies likewise involve decisions about decisions, and they may involve setting up organizations to do things that further affect decisions.

We can think of policy, therefore, as existing on at least three levels. There is first of all the policy of an individual. This is deeply involved with the individual's identity and the choice of identity. In a sense the choice of identity is itself a policy. Then we have policy at the level of organizations, in decisions both to form organizations and to guide them after they have been formed. These may be private organizations, but the concept is valid also for the suborganizations within government. The head of a bureau, for instance, may have a certain latitude with regard to policy, and the future will be a little different according to which policy is selected. Finally, there is a policy at the highest level of government which is made by a very complex process. It has as its background the general consensus on which all government rests, but this is sharpened and modified and put into more exact terms in the course of the processes by which powerful people make decisions. At this level policies may not be very explicit, they may not even be very consistent. Every decision maker, however, must have an underlying matrix of policy within which some decisions are more probable than others.

Personal policy with regard to a war-peace system varies greatly from individual to individual. At one end of the scale is the pacifist, whose policy is to abstain from violence in all personal relations and to refuse to accept any role which involves violence, such as that of a soldier. Pacifism in this sense is a bit like teetotalism or celibacy. That is, it is a rule of life involving certain taboos, just as having a full beard involves a rule of life with a taboo on shaving. In this sense pacifism is not a political philosophy, though it usually comes out of certain images of the world and certain evaluations of it, particularly those putting a very low political value on violence. It may involve simply a low value on political action of any kind, though this is by no means universal among pacifists. The Amish, for instance, who simply withdraw from the world and create their own culture with a minimum of contact with the world outside them, are an example of pacifism of this kind. Whether it is feasible or not of course depends on the nature of the society in which it is embedded. It has been feasible in this country for two or three hundred years. Sometimes this total pacifism breaks down, as in Russia under the first collectivization, when the Mennonites were largely destroyed by Stalin's fury. This however is a perfectly general principle, that the capacity of any species to survive depends upon its environment. Pacifism of a less withdrawn kind, like that of the Quakers in early Pennsylvania, involves serious moral dilemmas, but then we are never exempt from these no matter what personal policy we choose.

This is an area in which I have been deeply involved as an individual, as well as a social scientist. I hope I can look at it objectively as part of the great ecosystem of society. The personal experiences which lead into pacifism, like those which lead into alienation and the IRA, are apt to be special to the particular environment of the person. There is an interesting and somewhat unexplored field of study here. Even in my own case, I would find it hard to say what particular experiences of childhood convinced me at the age of fourteen to choose an identity which led me to becoming a Quaker. On reflection I think it may have been an almost unconscious sense that I had been deceived as a child with the patriotic fervor of the First World War. There is no destroyer of legitimacy more powerful than a sense of having been deceived and lied to. I have never felt free, however, to indulge in ethical judgment of those who choose other identities, except perhaps those whose identities involve deceit. Indeed I think I have always felt closer to the honest soldier than to the slippery peacemonger. It is a matter of individual policy and each must make his or her own, even though each will be affected by the surrounding environments and will have to choose the identity of a conformist or a nonconformist.

The overall effects of personal policy on society are hard to evaluate. Pacifists, for instance, have always been a very small group. They have sometimes been accused of bringing on a war by undermining deterrence, though it would be hard to find cases. Their influence in the delegitimation of war as an institution has possibly been large. Sometimes it takes only one child to say that the emperor has no clothes on. Where an institution is ripe for delegitimation a single person, such as Martin Luther King, can have an enormous impact.

At the opposite extreme from the pacifist we have the militarist, the person whose policy and identity involve the uncritical acceptance of war as a necessary social institution in which the individual wholeheartedly participates. It may be just as "moral" as pacifism, though it may also be subject to corruption by those who find war a legitimation of sadism and malevolence and an excuse for sexual license and theft. Between the two extremes is a whole spectrum of personal policy ranging from noncombatant service to quiet sabotage of the military activity (a surprising number of soldiers in the Korean War apparently did not fire their guns), to a grim and uneasy performance of a doubtfully moral and disagreeable duty, to the full-fledged militarist. The distribution of these personal policies in the population may be an important element in the ability of a nation, for instance, to conduct a war. There is no doubt that in Vietnam the United States was prevented from exercising more than a fraction of its potential military power because of the unpopularity of the war and the vocal and influential character of the dissidents. Here again the destruction of the legitimacy of President Johnson in the minds of many people who sensed they had been deceived, in that campaign utterances did not represent his true position, had some impact on the delegitimation of the whole operation.

The dream of the pacifists that "someday somebody will give a war and nobody will come" is perhaps unrealistic, but the impact of the delegitimation of war through personal policy must not be underestimated. War can be relegitimated, of course, by a sense of crisis, of deep threat to cherished values, and so on. In the dynamics of society we see kind of a seesaw between war weariness and delegitimation and war proneness and relegitimation, but as the costs of war become more onerous one suspects that the balance of the dynamics of legitimation will be on the side of peace.

Organizational policy with regard to peace involves a wide variety of organizations. At one end, again, we have the organizations of the peace movement—small, scattered, and often at odds with each other. Even in the peace movement peace is unstable, though the forms of conflict are very mild. A significant development of the twentieth century has been the rise of organizations for nonviolent resistance, even though these have usually been rather sporadic and short-lived. This is documented at great length in the work of Gene Sharp.[1] Gandhi and Martin Luther King, of course, are the best-known exponents, but there is by now a large history of organized nonviolence. It has frequently been very effective in achieving both national independence in the case of India and social change in the United States. It rests

1. Gene Sharp, *The Politics of Nonviolent Action* (Boston: Porter Sargent, 1973).

on a more holistic and integrated view of the social system than does conventional military theory. It exploits the integrative and legitimative factors in the system in a way that violent action—whether of internal war or of external war—inevitably fails to do. Nonviolence, however, is still part of the threat system, even when it involves nonsubmission to threats, for its power lies in the delegitimation of authoritative threat. Like every other social invention it can be abused, but it has the peculiar virtue that when it is abused it is seldom very powerful, for its power depends on the appeal to latent legitimacies and illegitimacies and unless these are present it will be powerless. Even when it provokes violence, as it occasionally does, the total situation is more likely to have a fruitful dynamic which will lead to ultimate integration than an initial appeal to violence is likely to produce. The power of Gandhi, for instance, lay in his ability to undermine the belief of the British in the legitimacy of their own empire. If the empire had not been an economic burden to them, as it almost certainly was, he might have been less successful. But economic burdens often exist for a very long time, supported by habit and vanity, unless their legitimacy can be destroyed.

Besides the peace movement, one must also look at the private organizations for supporting the institution of war, like the Navy League, the American Legion, and the lobbies of the arms manufacturers and war industry. In most societies these seem to be much more powerful than the organizations of the peace movement, perhaps because war involves people in an intense and sacrificing way seldom paralleled in the organizations of the peace movement. Here we again see the principle of the sacrifice trap. Imprisoning and exiling conscientious objectors usually increase their devotion to the peace movement and increase its legitimacy. The suffering and death of conscientious objectors, however, are small compared with the suffering and death of soldiers, and it is not surprising that this sacrifice creates a strong sense of identification with the military institutions. This is particularly true of rural people and working-class people, among whom the peace movement is very weak and for whom participation in war is often the most intense experience of their lives. The demand for spectacular sacrifice creates loyalty.

Then we come to the policies of the armed forces themselves, insofar as these have a latitude distinct from the policies of the government. Societies differ a good deal with regard to the power of the armed forces to determine their own policies. In the United States, for instance, the tradition of civilian control is very strong, though the real power of the civil government surfaces only occasionally—for instance, in President Truman's dismissal of MacArthur. In most but not all of the poor countries military dictatorship is the rule, though there are intermissions of civilian government. It is not always the case, however, that military government favors the military as an organization, for the cares and responsibilities of civil government may sometimes divert the military from military tasks and policy. It could well be that military and quasi-military organizations under a civilian government, like the CIA in the United States, actually have greater power over government policy than similar organizations in countries where there is officially a military dictatorship. This is very hard to estimate.

There is an increasing tendency for military people to be highly specialized professionals. They do develop something of a professional ethic. On the other hand, like other professionals they are not averse to expanding their power, influence, and income. In democratic societies, of course, the military budget is ultimately a decision of the legislature. The military have considerable power in the legislatures through their lobbying organizations. There is supposed to be one Pentagon lobbyist, for instance, for at least every two members of Congress, but their power is limited by the perceptions of legislators with regard to the international situation. The idea that countries have a large military budget because of the desire to prevent unemployment or to placate a sizable sector of the economy is largely an illusion, though it occasionally has elements of truth, especially for the projects of particularly powerful legislators.

On the whole the decisions about military budgets tend to be guided by perceptions of threat from abroad or of the general instability of the international system rather than by strictly domestic considerations. As we have seen in chapter 1, the hawks in the United States Congress, for instance, do not come from districts with a heavy percentage of war industry but, rather, from the South and from rural areas where the military ideology tends to be the moral norm. This does not rule out the fact that there are particular legislators with particular economic interests in the military organizations, but these will tend to be fairly helpless without an overall sense of threat to national security. It is not surprising that the military try to create a sense of national insecurity, for they benefit from this. Estimates made by the American military and the CIA of Russian armaments, for example, are far larger than the estimates made by the Stockholm International Peace Research Institute. This is a profound source of instability in the international system, for each nation tends to perceive the threat from another nation as greater than it actually is —hence each nation increases its own counterthreat accordingly.

Finally we come to the question of whether a national government could have a genuine and successful policy for promoting peace. Such a policy should not necessarily be judged by the criterion of 100 percent success. One of the things that probably militates against a peace policy being taken seriously is that it is not regarded in probabilistic terms as a design to diminish the probability of war but is always judged in absolute terms, so that a breakdown into war would discredit it completely. Another obstacle to a peace policy is the widespread feeling that the war-peace system is an essentially uncontrollable environment to which individual nations can react but which they cannot really govern any more than they can govern the weather. It is worth remembering, however, that depressions used to be called economic blizzards.

In the past, peace policy has been frustrated because of inadequate and oversimplified models of the international system which have prevented approaches to the problem based on refined, pointed, and piecemeal policies. The first great fallacy is the ancient classic that peace is guaranteed by a balance of power. Essentially this is a deterrence theory. It can produce temporary stability, particularly in a fairly bipolar situation. In a multiparty situation it becomes virtually impossible because of the probability of shifting alliances. This is the classic problem of the n-person game. The metaphor of the balance of power is a gross oversimplification of the complexity of the international system and the decision-making process within it.

There is an opposite theory that peace is preserved by a preponderance of power. There may be some cases in which this theory holds for a while, but it can also be shown to be unstable simply because of the sheer cost of maintaining predominance. Being a great power is extremely expensive and almost universally damaging to the economies of the countries which have this ambition, though the ambition itself often arises out of the past success of the economy. We could almost sum up the matter in the aphorism that wealth creates power and power destroys wealth. The impermanence of empire is one of the most striking phenomena in human history, and the occasional Pax Romana or Pax Britannica has been costly to the imperial power, fairly short-lived, and not all that peaceful. The Pax Americana, indeed, hardly ever got off the ground.

Another fallacy, which might be called the all-or-nothing fallacy, is that the only answer to war is a world government and the total destruction of national sovereignty. The existence of islands of stable peace among sovereign states suggests that world government is not absolutely necessary to peace. Furthermore, the constant tendency for federations to break up and even for federal states to undergo civil wars suggests that a federation is by no means a universal recipe for peace. A world government indeed would be so fantastically heterogeneous, particularly at the present low level of the sense of world community, that it would almost inevitably either degenerate into a tyranny of one party or group over the others or break up into world civil strife. The analogy of 1789 often used by world government advocates is a very dubious one. The thirteen colonies had a reasonably homogeneous culture, a common language, a common heritage, a common enemy, and, in the 1860s, nearly fourscore years and ten of a common history. But all the apparatus of federal government could not keep the union from coming apart in the civil war because of its cultural heterogeneity.

The tendency in the last thirty years indeed has been toward the breakup of empires and federations and the creation of large numbers of new sovereign states, many of which are extremely heterogeneous with completely arbitrary boundaries, especially in Africa. Even within the old sovereign states separatist movements have increased in strength, such as the Welsh and the Scots in Britain, the Basques and the Bretons in France, the French in Quebec, the Maya in Mexico, the Bengalis in Bangladesh—one of the few separatist movements that was successful—the Ibo in Nigeria, who spearheaded the abortive Biafran rebellion, and so on all around the world. One wonders how long the Soviet Union can hold out as the last relic of the nineteenth-century empires in the face of its enormous heterogeneity.

It seems, therefore, as if we are going to have to look for dissociative solutions to the problem of peace rather than associative ones for a long time to come. Indeed there is much to be said for this from the point of view of the internal policy of a nation. The small, homogeneous nations are much easier to manage and are less likely to make serious mistakes in internal policy. The one institution that looks like a successful federation is the European Common Market. But it does not look as if this is going to lead into political federation, and it may be that it is in special-purpose organizations like this that we are going to find the associative solutions rather than in some overall federal system of regional or even world government.

Another peace policy which turns out to be an illusion is the Wilsonian doctrine of collective security. The idea behind this was a kind of Hobbesian social contract of all against the aggressor. This indeed was the theory of the League of Nations. It foundered first because of the difficulty of getting nations to agree on the perception and the definition of aggression. What A perceives as aggression B perceives as defense. The second difficulty was what Garrett Hardin has called a "tragedy of the commons" situation in which there were neither clear-cut property rights in the system of mutual defense nor any community organization with allocative power. It may be that the failure of the League of Nations was partly due to bad luck as well as to bad management and poor organization, for it did have to face a very exceptional situation in Hitler, who might almost be described as a thousand-year flood of the international system, that is, a rather unlikely event that came off and from which we very extensively overlearned. The problem of the sustainability of a system under improbable catastrophe is of course a very real one, but a system which failed under an improbable catastrophe might have been successful under luckier circumstances. Nevertheless, the whole Wilsonian view of the international system was a highly oversimplified model of aggression and collective resistance to it, and the system needed a considerable amount of good luck to succeed.

The view I am propounding is a modest, somewhat piecemeal, but one hopes a realistic approach to a long-run peace policy capable of surviving disappointments and occasional breakdowns. It is more capable of long-run growth than the grand schemes which have little chance of coming into being or could easily prove catastrophically unstable even if they did come into being. It looks at the problem in terms of both reducing strain on the system and increasing its strength to resist strain, the latter depending a great deal on convention and taboo. The object is not to produce a system of infinite strength capable of resisting all strain but to simply reduce strain and increase strength and so increase the likelihood that the system will resist strain.

The general strategy emphasizes not only positive social contracts such as treaties, agreements, unions, and world political organizations but also what might be called negative social contracts, that is, agreements which may be quite tacit and undocumented to take certain things off agendas. An agreement to do nothing is often much easier than an agreement to do something. We are so hypnotized by the power of positive thinking and the supposed necessity to be active that we underestimate the enormous power of taboo and passivity. One recalls an apocryphal story that Eisenhower once said to Dulles, "Don't just do something, stand there."

One sometimes feels that apathy is the greatest power in the world, and apathy in the doing of evil has a lot to recommend it. It is a nice question, of course, as to whether apathy can be promoted by positive policy. It is certainly hard to make a vigorous speech about getting out the apathy. On the other hand, a positive and explicit policy toward tacit understanding is entirely feasible. Thomas Schelling has shown indeed that there can be an enormous amount of agreement in the absence of communication among bargainers.[2] We assume far too easily that everything has to be explicit. A richer and more realistic model of the social and international system would reveal the enormous importance of what is not said, not signed, but quietly taken as a rule of behavior. Without this element in social life, indeed, all societies would fall apart almost overnight. What I am looking for here is an almost half-conscious peace policy, communicated by nods, smiles, and raised eyebrows, and an atmosphere of intercourse which underlies the agreements, treaties, and declarations and often makes all the difference between failure and success.

The first plank in such a policy would be the removal of national boundaries from political agendas, except under circumstances of strong mutual agreement. A very large proportion of international war arises from dissatisfaction with existing boundaries and attempts to change them. The internal peace among the states of the United States arises more from the fact that the sheer absurdity of the state boundaries virtually takes them off everybody's agenda than from the existence of a federal apparatus which could resolve these disputes if they arose. In serious disputes among the states the federal government would probably be helpless. It is a situation in which the strength of the system is not very great, as the Civil War showed, but a convention of behavior lessens the strain and so preserves the peace. Federalists are apt to mistake a lack of strain for strength.

There are two situations in which boundaries get re-

2. Thomas C. Schelling, "Bargaining, Communication, and Limited War," *Journal of Conflict Resolution* 1 (March 1957): 19.

moved from agendas. One is where the boundaries are natural and correspond to cultural boundaries, so each country is fairly homogeneous and does not have irredenta, that is, populations which identify with it but live in neighboring countries. One could almost interpret the two world wars of the twentieth century in Europe as very costly methods of establishing reasonably homogeneous states. The European states of today are far more homogeneous than they were in 1914, when we had the great heterogeneous empires of Austria-Hungary and Russia as well as innumerable irredenta all over the map. Today, virtually all the Germans are living in one of the two Germanies; nearly all the French are in France, though some non-French are in France; nearly all the Italians are in Italy, though unfortunately Italy contains a little clump of Austrians in the Tyrol; and nearly all the Poles are in Poland. There are Hungarians in Romania, but this is because Romanians occupy a donut with Hungarians in the hole. This makes cultural boundaries very hard to draw. The present situation means that the strain on boundary change has been much reduced in Europe, though the recent migration of populations from poor European countries, mostly of the south, including Turkey, to the richer, northern countries has created potential difficulties for the future. Similarly the immigration of Jamaicans, Pakistanis, and others into Britain has created certain internal heterogeneities. These people, however, are not irredenta because they do not create boundary problems.

In Africa we have the opposite situation. Like the states of the United States, the boundaries of the new African countries are so preposterous that nearly everybody shrinks from the attempt to change them. They are leftovers from the colonial era, resulting from the geographical errors of the Europeans, and they divide many cultural and linguistic groups. Nevertheless, there has been virtually no international war in Africa in the last generation, with the exception of Egypt and the Middle East, which is of course another part of the forest altogether. There have been a number of bloody internal wars—for instance, in Nigeria, the Sudan, the Congo (now Zaïre), and Burundi—but incidents involving international frontiers have been quite minor, until the ominous Ethiopia-Somalia war in 1977. It is much to be hoped that this relative international peace will continue. Certainly any attempt at this point to rectify the African boundaries in general would result in total chaos.

In South America boundary problems have died down since the nineteenth century, though there are still some subterranean ones in, for example, Bolivia, Peru, Chile, and Paraguay. In Asia the situation is very complex because nearly all the Asian countries have a considerable degree of cultural heterogeneity. India is a vast patchwork of potential nations, and it is still something of an open question as to whether it can sustain enough unity to avoid splitting up. If it did split up the populations themselves might be better off, with more manageable states. Burma, Thailand, and to a lesser extent Vietnam are also very heterogeneous. China is more homogeneous, though Canton is very different from Peking, and China has some 50 million non-Chinese peoples. Like the U.S.S.R. it also represents a nineteenth-century empire, at least in Tibet and the far west. The Soviet Union, as we have noted, is extremely heterogeneous. The Chinese-Russian border indeed is an important potential source of conflict. It represents historically the high-water mark of czarist expansion.

A second aspect of peace policy would be the consistent pursuit of what Professor Charles Osgood has called "Graduated and Reciprocated Initiative in Tension-Reduction (GRIT)."[3] This involves a conscious image of the international system as a process of action and reaction in a constant, unstable, dynamic succession of decisions, acts, induced decisions, induced acts, and so on indefinitely. This view of the world downplays the concept of equilibrium which has so often dominated thinking on these matters, though it would not deny that there is a process of this kind that can reach at least a temporary equilibrium which is hard to shift. Any equilibrium, however, is an invitation to think up new patterns of behavior which would set off the process of change again. The process of détente between the United States and the Soviet Union, which goes back at least to Eisenhower and Krushchev and began perhaps with Khrushchev's doctrine of peaceful coexistence, has many aspects of the GRIT process. Its history indeed still remains to be written. These processes are by no means new and they go back a long way in human history, though they have not often been recognized as a species of process in the general field of the learning of peace.

The GRIT process begins by some rather specific, perhaps even dramatic, statement or act directed at a potential enemy (like Sadat's 1977 visit to Israel), intended to be reassuring and perhaps even naming or implying some act which might be taken in response, though this

3. Charles E. Osgood, *An Alternative to War or Surrender* (Urbana: University of Illinois Press, 1962).

is somewhat dangerous if the suggested act is too specific. If the potential enemy responds, then a third act by the first party, a fourth by the second party, and so on could produce a dynamic of adjusting national images until the images become compatible. If there is an equilibrium to this process, it is to move toward compatibility of national images. And this, one suspects, can be spelled out in much greater detail than is usually done now. Most negotiation and interaction at the international systems level are conducted in an atmosphere of implicit national images, which can often be quite illusory. An exchange of information in these matters would play somewhat the same kind of role in the international system that the marriage counselor does in family conflict, where the communication system frequently produces mutually false images of the other party. In any conflict of two parties, A and B, there are at least four images involved—A's image of A, A's image of B, B's image of A, and B's image of B—and these can be very different. It by no means follows of course that, if A's image of B is the same as B's image of B, and B's image of A is the same as A's image of A, the conflict will be resolved. But, if these images are widely different, unnecessary and unreasonable conflict is likely to follow.

A peace dynamic is not enough, important as it is. At some point the dynamic must become explicit in a peace policy, expressed first perhaps in some dramatic public statement and act. This could be started by a single nation, preferably one of the superpowers. It could be embodied in a United Nations declaration or a treaty to which all nations would be invited to assent. The first step could be a public statement on the part of a major government, affirming the concept of stable peace and establishing it as the major goal of national policy. The main function of a statement or a manifesto is to create hypocrisy, which is a powerful agent of social change, for when actual policy is perceived to be too different from the professed statement a fulcrum for change toward the profession is provided. Manifestoes, however, tend to be ineffective unless they result in an organization. Neither the Declaration of Independence nor the Communist Manifesto would have come to much if they had not produced organizations to embody them and propagate them.

The first step in a peace policy after the manifesto, therefore, should be to set up a Department of Peace within the government with a number of missions. It should educate the public and the government in the meaning of stable peace and in the dynamics of peace policy through schools, the press, radio, television, publications, and so on. It should develop a research institute in the techniques of achieving stable peace, part of which might well be an in-house operation, patterned perhaps on the Stockholm International Peace Research Institute, and part of which might be a foundation, like the National Science Foundation, to encourage research in the universities and elsewhere. Part of this task should be the continuing collection and improvement of data on the conflictual aspects of the world system. Part of this would be a continuing program in the description and dynamics of national images, with a view to increasing their compatibility. There would also be a program like the present Arms Control and Disarmament Agency, one would hope on a greatly expanded scale.

A third element in peace policy would involve the serious exploration of both the theory and the practice of nonviolent responses to threats of violence, together with the formation of organizations to develop these nonviolent activities. Nonviolence is by no means a universal panacea, but it is one of the instruments of human betterment which deserves to be more clearly understood and prepared for, with regard to both its limits and its potentialities. There is now a large and serious literature on this subject.[4] It can no longer be regarded as an eccentricity of saints. It should be part of the curriculum of every military academy. There should be institutes for its study and organizations to teach it. It represents an expansion of the agenda or repertory of the decision maker in many different types of social systems. It may be, as a high official in the Indian defense establishment once said to me, that it is much more suitable for aggression than for defense, more suitable for instance to create wanted social change than to defend against unwanted social change. This, however, needs to be investigated. What is most urgent is that nonviolence should be taken seriously.

A fourth aspect of a policy for peace would involve the piecemeal transformation of the role of the military in the direction of soldiers without enemies. This is already underway in such experiences as the United Nations forces in the Middle East, Cyprus, the Congo, and so on and in such organizations as General Rikhye's International Peace Academy.[5] This is a real social invention. Its use so far has been very small compared with

4. See especially Sharp, *The Politics of Nonviolent Action*, p. 413.
5. See the publications of the International Peace Academy, 777 United Nations Plaza, New York, N.Y. 10017.

the enormous expenditures on soldiers with enemies and the national armed forces. Nevertheless, it represents a logical expansion of the role and the culture of the military in a direction that has enormous potential for the future. Whether existing military organizations can be transformed in this way may be doubted. The concept of the enemy is so fundamental to the military ethos, legitimacy, and morale that the new concept would undoubtedly be perceived as a threat to the existing military subcultures. It is significant, however, that much of the initiative in the development of the soldiers without enemies organizations comes from military men themselves such as Harbottle, who was the director of the United Nations forces in Cyprus.[6] It may be that transformations of this kind would be welcomed by intelligent and sensitive members of the military who are disturbed by the fact that the traditional military ethos and culture have increasingly become a threat to human welfare in the altered state of military technology and the new conditions of the world. The destructive impact of the Vietnam War on the morale and legitimacy of the United States military establishment is the warning sign that the traditional military ethos may be on the point of collapse and that something new is needed.

A fifth plank in a peace policy would be national policies aimed at strengthening the structure of world political organizations, particularly intergovernmental organizations. The international nongovernmental organizations are only marginally within the purview of

6. Michael Harbottle, *The Impartial Soldier* (London: Oxford University Press, 1970).

national policy, though there are problems with regard to permitting their operation within the nation. The great hole in the structure of world political organizations is the absence of any organization for negotiating disarmament. The United States and the Soviet Union have been making rather halfhearted attempts at SALT talks, but these have done nothing to reduce the general level of armaments or even reduce them at the points where they might cause the most trouble, namely at the borders. A United Nations Disarmament Organization, which would have the delightful acronym of UNDO, could act as a kind of marriage counselor in flitting back and forth among various decision makers, clarifying understandings, widening agendas, and removing obstacles to agreement. It could also play a role in policing, in inspecting agreements once they are obtained, and in monitoring the whole world war industry, as the Swedish International Peace Research Institute does now in a small way.

Bilateral disarmament negotiations are extraordinarily difficult in the absence of any mediating agency. It is not surprising that they have accomplished so little. There are many places in the world where partial and incomplete disarmaments, the moving of troops back from the frontier, inspection, and cooperation among armed forces could bring about both a lessening of the strain and an increase in the strength of the system. The effectiveness of a disarmament organization would obviously be determined partly by its own personnel, partly by the support given it by the various governments. That it is desperately needed can hardly be questioned. The almost inevitable proliferation of nuclear weapons and the grave potential instability of a multipolar system make the necessity for a United Nations Disarmament Organization all the greater.

I would also like to see a United Nations Spying Organization which would spy on everybody and publish the results immediately. Secrecy in the international system is a very important cause in itself of strain. It produces extraordinary misapprehensions and illusions. Indeed, there is no segment of the social system in which the images of the world in the minds of the powerful decision makers are more deliberately formed by biased and inaccurate information. Even if one could not have a United Nations Spying Organization in the present state of mythology of the international system, one could at least have a United Nations Intelligence Organization for the study and publication of social indicators of strain on the system and, with more difficulty, its strength. With present techniques of the analysis of events data and content analysis, a great deal could be done to present the current picture of the international system as it moves from day to day in terms which are relatively free from bias and which are based on objective sampling. This one hopes would supplement and perhaps eventually supplant the vast apparatus of biased information collected and processed through spies, diplomats, state departments, and foreign offices.

Public intelligence organizations indeed are needed in many spheres of life to offset the inevitable corruption of information as it flows up through a large organization to the powerful decision makers. A friend of mine once visited a top official on the seventh floor of the State Department and found him sorting out the telegrams to go to the president, with only the favorable

for about twenty-five years. It has frequently been a discouraging and disheartening business, harder to finance I think than almost any other operation around a university. In part this reflects the strange limbo in which we find ourselves today, in that neither peace nor war is legitimate. The attitudes left over from a system of unstable peace make it hard for people to believe that concentrated, serious scientific endeavor could go into moving the world toward stable peace. The peace research movement itself is by no means a united enterprise. Nevertheless, over the years it has produced a substantial body of literature. Much of this is exploratory and tentative. We cannot claim any great successes like DNA or plate tectonics. It is absurd to suppose, however, that the social system in general and the international system in particular are not fit subjects for careful scientific inquiry. Our information system can be enormously improved and so can our theoretical structures. In light of the enormous urgency of the problem and the threat which war now represents to the continued existence of the human race, one would think that our strategy for the allocation of research resources would give peace research a high priority instead of the meager pittances it now gets. These problems will be explored more fully in the next chapter.

These seven proposals are modest, they are all attainable within a reasonable amount of time, and they constitute a direction of change. Perhaps the greatest enemy of the human race is the very widespread feeling that its problems must be solved once and for all by some dramatic coup. This is not what the universe is like. The human race is a continuation of a great evolutionary process which has been going on in this part of the universe for billions of years and which will probably go on somewhere in the universe for more billions of years. In evolution there are no sure things, there is no equilibrium, there are only constant mutation and ecological interaction. The quest for peace must be part of an evolutionary process. It will suffer endless reversals and disappointments. What is important is that it has a direction in terms of human betterment. The evolutionary process is punctuated by catastrophes, but the process itself has always survived. Evolution is essentially a process of learning. A good idea or an ideal is like an empty niche in an ecosystem—something will eventually move into it. Just as the genetic structure of the earth learned to make an eye in human organisms and to make space labs, it will someday learn to make peace. It is a painful process and we only learn from failure, but there is an asymmetry in it: error can be found out, truth cannot. Evil when detected is rejected; good when detected is not. It is this asymmetry which gives evolution a direction, a time's arrow. In our own time the arrow points clearly and unequivocally toward peace.

5. Research for peace

Research, as a specialized human activity in information gathering and knowledge production, may well have begun in the international system as ancient rulers sent spies and diplomats to collect information about potential enemies and so improve their own image of their political environment. Caleb and Joshua and their associates who were sent by Moses to spy out the land of Canaan[1] are an early record of a research team, though this was more war research than peace research. The number of people and the amount of resources devoted to research have increased almost exponentially in the last few hundred years and are now a major element of society, particularly in the developed countries. We put more than a third of our resources into what has been called the knowledge industry.

There are at least three levels of human activity devoted to the increase of knowledge, that is, the improvement of our images of the world in ways that bring them closer to the outside reality. The first of these proc-

1. Numbers 13.

esses produces what might be called folk knowledge, the knowledge we acquire in the ordinary business of life. This is knowledge mainly of our immediate environment—our own household, our family, the town where we live, the people with whom we come into continuous contact. We all have an image of the geography of our own town, for instance, which is constantly being revised in the course of our experience as we go to places we thought were there and find they have changed: a bus route has been altered, the post office has been moved, a two-way street has become one-way, and so on. Folk knowledge is usually very accurate because the feedbacks from error are rapid. Folk knowledge of other persons may be less accurate than knowledge of places, as persons are so complicated that there is ample room for misunderstanding and misinterpretation of signals.

The second form of cognitive activity might be called literary knowledge. It begins before writing with the development of folktales and specialized poets and singers who transmit the accumulated folklore and history of their group. With the coming of writing, literary knowledge expands enormously. It is represented by records, histories, newspapers, diplomatic cables, reports of spies, internal memoranda, and so on. Literary knowledge may originate somewhere in direct personal experience, but this experience is translated into language which is then retransmitted and retranslated many times. Literary knowledge is much more extensive than folk knowledge. It is necessary if we are to have knowledge of things beyond our own immediate personal experience, but what it gains in extension it tends to lose in accuracy and feedback. An error in our image of the town where we live is easily corrected. An error in a report or a document tends to be perpetuated forever. Literary knowledge, therefore, tends to be judged by internal consistency rather than by direct testing. This, however, easily leads to the perpetuation of error, for consistency may simply mean being consistent with our preconceived notions. Everybody who receives literary knowledge tends to filter it through a preconceived image of the world, and the things that are inconsistent with that image are usually rejected, unless they have extraordinary power and cogency. In early times bearers of bad news were often killed so they did not have to be believed.

Literary knowledge is of great importance in the international system, which explains perhaps why the international system is so remarkably prone to bad decisions. The world images of powerful decision makers tend to be corrupted by their own power, by their own preconceptions, and by the fear in which they are held by those who provide them with information. Consequently each decision maker is operating in a different imaginary universe. It is not surprising that decisions clash or that decisions frequently turn out to be catastrophic for the decision makers themselves.

The third cognitive process involves the production of scientific knowledge. This is an attempt by the scientific community to develop knowledge of large systems beyond our personal experience, extending indeed to the very bounds of the universe. Because of this, scientific knowledge almost certainly has a larger percentage of error than folk knowledge, but it also involves processes by which this percentage of error is systematically reduced through careful and instrumented observation, through making continuous, well-planned records, through experiments by which particular propositions can be tested in artificial situations, and through logical mathematical methods by which theoretical systems can be tested for inconsistency. Whereas literary knowledge rests heavily on the authority of the writer and the transmitter, scientific knowledge is an attempt to return to the immediacy of folk knowledge on a larger scale and in larger systems.

Science walks on two legs, observation and experiment, and all the sciences contain certain mixtures of these. Some, like astronomy, must rely more on observation and others, like chemistry, rely much more on experiment. The scientific revolution, the roots of which go back to early civilizations, developed into an explosive growth of knowledge which may be dated from Copernicus some five hundred years ago. Instrumentation has played a very important role in this process; the development of the telescope, the microscope, the camera, and electrical instruments has enormously expanded the observational capacity of the human race beyond what can be provided by our naked senses. This has forced us into constant readjustments of our images of the world and the universe. Quantification has been an important element in this expansion of observation, though contrary to popular belief science does not simply involve reducing everything to numbers. It also involves topological description and qualitative estimates.

The movement of science has been characterized by surges in which particular aspects of the universe have been suddenly illuminated and our knowledge has expanded very rapidly in a short time. We associate a great surge in astronomy with Copernicus, Kepler, Tycho Brahe, and Galileo; in mechanics with Newton; in chemistry with Dalton; in biology with Darwin; and so on. In the twentieth century we have seen such surges in physics with Einstein, in economics with Keynes, in molecular biology with Crick and Watson, in geology with plate tectonics, and in astronomy with radio and x-ray receivers. There is a common view that physics developed first, biology next, and the social sciences next, with physics being the most successful, biology next, and the social sciences still in their infancy. This is largely an illusion. Economics, for instance, is older than chemistry, which was still struggling with phlogiston at the time of Adam Smith. Furthermore, the ranking of the sciences in terms of their security, that is, the likelihood of large changes in their image of the universe, depends mainly on the size of the sample which they have been able to take relative to the total universe of their discourse. On these grounds the social sciences are probably the most secure and the least likely to be subject to radical change, with the possible exception of psychology, whereas physics and astronomy have probably sampled only a small part of their total universe of 20 billion years and may be subject to very radical changes in the future.

Peace research is an intellectual movement, mainly within the social sciences, to apply the methods of science to problems of conflict, to war and peace, and to the improvement of these processes. As a self-conscious discipline and an "invisible college" it is not much more than twenty-five years old. A book by Theodore Lentz, *Towards the Science of Peace*, published in 1952, is an important landmark in the origin of the movement. On a more sporadic basis, of course, the movement goes back a long time and it inherits a long tradition of philosophical, historical, and literary studies of war and peace and a classical literature in many societies in the study of international law and political philosophy. Thinkers such as Erasmus, Grotius, Kant, William Penn, and so on represent a long history of human thought and concern about the problems of war and peace.

Almost every movement from literary and philosophical knowledge into science has been accompanied by improvements in instrumentation. The impact of the telescope and now of radio and x-ray receivers in astronomy, and the microscope and now the electron microscope in biology, can hardly be exaggerated. In the social sciences the twentieth century has seen a substantial improvement in instrumentation through the development of sample surveys, improved censuses, national income statistics, social indicators, and so on. This resulted first in a substantial improvement in the historical record, just as the telescope did in astronomy. We see this most dramatically perhaps in economic data, where before 1929 a few long, historical price series, tax data, and international trade data collected through customs were almost all that was available. Since 1929 in the United States, and somewhat later in other countries, we have national income statistics that give us year by year, quarter by quarter, a continuing picture of the main components of the economy. The taxonomy is far from perfect, and there are many things we do not know, but still the improvement is of an order of magnitude beyond what we had before, and it has had a profound impact on economic policy. We cannot imagine an American president now proposing a tax increase in the middle of a great depression, as Herbert Hoover did in 1932 when unemployment was 25 percent. We are still weak on information on capital structures and very weak on information with regard to distributional impacts, but these we hope will be improved in the next generation. The movement to develop social indicators has been less successful than the improvement in economic indicators, simply because of the great complexity and the difficulties of measurement in the noneconomic aspects of human behavior and organization. The measuring rod of money gives economics a certain advantage in quantification, though often this quantification may be deceptive, for reality is a multidimensional structure which defies description in any simple numerical terms.

Indexing and the interpretation of indexes remain crucial problems in the social sciences. The reality outside us consists of very large, multidimensional structural patterns, but we have a strong urge to know whether a particular change in them represents an increase or a decrease in some significant aggregate property. Aggregate properties, however, are always misleading unless we are aware of the heterogeneous structure which they are attempting to describe. Thus, we measure the growth of the body by an aggregate of weight without regard to whether this is brain or muscle or fat. Similarly, we represent the aggregate output of society by the GNP without regard to the fact that growth in the GNP may represent increased pollution, wasteful government expenditure, or increased weapons production. We represent the growth of population by a single number without regard to whether this indicates an increase in the incompetent or the disabled or the dependent. We represent inflation by an increase in the price level without regard to the fact that this always involves changes in the relative price structure, with some prices rising faster than others, some perhaps even falling. We aggregate the total amount of energy used by a society without regard to the fact that this is in many different forms and has many different uses, the structure of which may change. Even stability in any of these indexes may mask large changes in the structure which underlies them, and we always have to be aware of this. This does not mean that the indicators are useless; in fact, they are extremely useful, but they must be utilized with great care.

There seems to be some tendency in scientific disciplines to oscillate between what might be called the bibliography phase and the textbook phase. In the first of these there is a great intellectual ferment, a lot of publication, and large bibliographies emerge. There are perhaps two tests of a discipline in this phase: one, does it have a bibliography and, two, can you give an examination in it? By both of these tests peace research is a well-developed discipline, with an extensive bibliography, and if anyone would like to take an examination in it I would be happy to give one to test the mastery of the bibliography. In the textbook phase the intellectual ferment has produced a moderately homogeneous brew which can be summarized in a textbook. The conflict and peace studies discipline, as it has increasingly come to be called, has not yet reached this stage, but I would expect it to do so in the next ten years. It has established itself as a field of study in colleges and universities, where there are now more than fifty institutions offering programs in this area.

Another characteristic of a discipline in its first phase is the development of journals and societies. On this score also it is clear that peace research is a rising discipline. The United Nations collects data on peace research scholars, institutes, and publications. In 1973, for instance, fourteen countries—two in North America, ten in Europe, and two in the rest of the world—reported 297 scholars, 78 institutes, and 483 publications. Of these, the United States accounted for 70 scholars, 43 institutes, and 89 publications. There is now a considerable number of scientific journals in the field. The oldest perhaps are the *Journal of Conflict Resolution*, now published at Yale University, and the *Journal of Peace Research*, now published in Oslo. There is an International Peace Research Association which meets biennially. It is about fourteen years old, and it publishes the *International Peace Research Newsletter*. Its American counterpart is the Consortium on Peace Research, Education, and Development, which is nearly ten years old and coordinates the work of a substantial group of scholars.

The peace research community is not only international, it is highly interdisciplinary. In an area like this it is not always easy to identify the discipline of a writer, yet a rough estimate suggests that about 20 percent are sociologists, another 20 percent are political scientists, about 10 percent are psychologists and social psychologists, and the rest are educators, physicists, biologists, economists, philosophers, historians, theologians, lawyers, military scientists, and anthropologists. The content of peace research, of course, is much less interdisciplinary than the wide variety of its participants might suggest. Political scientists tend to do political science, sociologists sociology, economists economics, and this should not surprise us. Peace research is an interdiscipline rather than a discipline. It does not have the homogeneity of such older disciplines as economics or sociology. Nevertheless, one can detect the beginnings of a common theoretical structure which tends to be imposed on it by the subset of the real social system with which it primarily works. If conflict and peace studies is a reasonable subset of the real world, we should certainly expect that whatever structure and homogeneity it may have will be incorporated into the models with which we try to understand it.

One problem in the taxonomy of the sciences can cause a little trouble if it is not understood. All the sciences consist of intersecting sets. There are, for instance, interstitial disciplines like biochemistry and social psychology, and any applied science will intersect with a large number of the more pure sciences. The term "conflict and peace studies" suggests that there is a discipline in the general study of conflict and its resolution. Indeed, the French have a name for it—"polémologie." Conflict is a universal phenomenon in social systems; it exists within the individual, within families, in all organizations, between individuals, between organizations, between states, and so on. All these cases exhibit both similarities and differences, but it can certainly be argued that the similarities are great enough so that conflict studies is a useful discipline for studying conflict wherever it occurs. Economics, for instance, revolves around the phenomenon of exchange or the production, consumption, and transfer of exchangeables, and it could be argued that conflict studies is just as much a discipline with a large common theoretical base and a broad application as is economics. In its compara-

tive aspect it studies the differences between various
fields of conflict.

We also have a discipline of international studies
which takes the international system as its field. The
international system consists of the national states and
their dependencies, particularly that part of their activity which concerns their relations with each other. It also
includes the international governmental organizations,
centering around the United Nations, as well as international nongovernmental organizations, including international business organizations. In the broad sense it
includes any activity which crosses national boundaries
—communications, tourism, and so on. Conflict is an important part of this system, based as it is to a large extent
on mutual threat, but it is by no means all of it and
there are many nonconflictual elements. There is a large
intersection, therefore, between the field of international studies and the field of peace and conflict studies.
Each field also has parts which do not belong to this intersection, especially the nonconflictual parts of the international system and the noninternational parts of the
conflict system. Peace research, in the narrow sense of
the study of peace as a phase of the international system,
contrasting with the opposite phase of war, occupies
mainly the intersection between international studies
and conflict studies. But the boundaries are by no means
clear, and in a larger sense one could almost argue that
peace research ought to be the union of these two sets
rather than their intersection, for even conflict cannot be
understood except in the setting of the very large, nonconflictual element in the social system.

Another set of problems involves peace research as an

applied discipline, like, shall we say, industrial relations or black studies. In any applied field the question always arises, what is it applied to and who is it applied for? An applied field always implies a value structure, in that some things are judged to be better than others. Then the purpose of the applied field is to increase our knowledge of the dynamic processes of the real world to the point where we can more skillfully move the system from bad to better rather than from bad to worse.

In the applied field of conflict studies the value problems are quite difficult and create considerable conflict in themselves. We are most likely to reach agreement on instrumental values, that is, things which are valued because they give us a generalized power of achieving a variety of other things about which there may be disagreement. In conflict studies the best-recognized instrumental value would be the minimization of the cost of conflict. All conflict involves some cost in the sense that it absorbs resources that might be used for other things, and the conflict itself—whether nonviolent or violent—involves diminishing the welfare of the opponent. The cost is very clear in violent conflict, where resources are used by each party to destroy the goods of the other, but in a more subtle way this may also be true of nonviolent conflict, where the withholding of a consent imposes a cost on those who would benefit by the consent. Conflict behavior is, of course, determined by the perception of costs and benefits, and these may be unrealistic. One of the major functions of conflict studies is to uncover those situations in which victory will not benefit the victor, though each party to the conflict thinks it will or the conflict would not continue. A constant task of conflict research, therefore, is to unmask illusory conflicts. This is not to say, of course, that all conflicts are illusory, and it may be that there are conflicts in which research might reveal that what was previously thought to be illusory in fact is real and so might intensify the conflict.

There is a marked difference between the value of lowering the cost of conflict and the value of winning. This would certainly be one way to describe the difference between peace research and war research—peace research being concerned with diminishing the cost of conflict no matter who wins and war research being devoted to winning no matter what the costs. In the real world both these values tend to be mixed; it muddies the situation. But where mud is a property of the real world there is no point in having models that deny it.

There has been an important controversy within the peace research movement between what might be called the narrow view which stresses the importance of negative peace, that is, peace as the absence of war in the international system, and what might be called the broad view which stresses positive peace, or the elimination of structural violence. This latter view is particularly associated with a distinguished Norwegian peace researcher, Johan Galtung. There is some tendency for the broad view to be European, the narrow view to be American, though there are many exceptions to this rule. Galtung began by defining structural violence as any structure in society which produced expectations of life below the normal expectation of, say, seventy years or so. The concept has rapidly expanded, however, as one slightly unfriendly critic remarked, "to define structural violence as anything that Galtung didn't like." To some extent the dispute is a semantic one as to how peace research should be defined, though there is a substantive question involved as to whether the processes which produce peace in the narrow sense are similar enough to those which produce a diminution of structural violence, however defined, so these can be usefully put together in a single discipline.

A consensus seems to be emerging that peace research is a loosely defined subset of a much larger area of inquiry which I call normative science. This is inquiry, by the methods and the ethic of the scientific community, into human valuations and their coordination, into such questions as what do we mean by things going from bad to better rather than from bad to worse and, if we can come to some limitation of this meaning, what processes in society actually move things from bad to better rather than from bad to worse? This of course is a very large study. It includes things like poverty, oppression, the illegitimate use of power, defenses against abuses of power, distribution and equity, and so on. It is clear that peace research in the narrow sense is a subset of this larger subject, though a very important one, particularly in the modern era where failure to solve the problem of negative peace may result in an enormous worsening of the human condition and a very large diminution of positive peace in any sense of the word.

There is a curiously vague boundary here between peace research and what might be called war research, not so much at the level of research in weapons development—which is clearly war research and takes such an inordinate amount of intellectual and human resources—but in what is often called strategic studies, which is the social science approach to the "how to win" problem. Actually the difference in basic values between the peace researchers and the war researchers makes less difference than might be thought to the actual content of the research.[2] This is presumably because both groups of researchers are investigating certain aspects of the real world and, while values are part of the real world and certainly change it, there is also a very large segment of the real world which is independent of the values of the researchers. The values of the researchers may filter their perceptions of the real world, but nevertheless the real world has a constant tendency to break through our prejudices about it, so it is not surprising that honest researchers (and we assume that most of them are) who approach a similar segment of the real world with different values may come out with a considerable similarity in their factual results. The conclusions as to what is optimum behavior may still be very different, for that depends on the values applied.

Historically, a great deal of the psychological impetus for the peace research enterprise came from somewhat dissatisfied members of the peace movement who happened to be social scientists and who perhaps felt that, while the peace movement provided a very legitimate demand for peace, it did not provide much of a supply. It was hoped that the application of the social sciences to these problems could be fruitful in guiding a demand for peace toward the supply, that is, toward those actual policies and decisions which are most likely to promote peace. In spite of its strong connections with the peace

2. See Kenneth E. Boulding and Elise Boulding, "The Homogeneity of International Studies: A Preliminary Analysis of the Content of Journals in the Field of International Studies," paper presented at a UNESCO General Conference, Paris, July 21–26, 1969.

movement, however, the peace research enterprise is not necessarily pacifist in the usual sense of the word, meaning individuals for whom violence is taboo. Consequently, the findings of peace research are likely to have usefulness even for the people who reject the values which may have given rise to it. The reverse is also true: the findings of the war researchers may have some considerable application in leading pacifists to more realistic political expressions of their personal values.

The three great tasks of any scientific discipline are, first, the formulation of theoretical structures; second, the development of a system of data collection in that subset of the real world with which the discipline is concerned; and, third, the application of the data to the testing of theories and the theories to the improvement of data. On all three counts peace research stands out as a lively but somewhat immature discipline. There is not a single, universally recognized, internally coherent body of theory. When there is, the discipline will have arrived at the textbook stage. There are indications that this stage is not very far off and that there is actually a considerable body of theory which exhibits at least a moderate amount of coherence. Surprisingly the theory that is emerging is also highly relevant to normative science in general, and we may indeed end up with peace theory as a section of the general history of normative science.

Several pieces of the pattern are beginning to fit together. One is game theory, particularly the theory of non-zero-sum games. Game theory was developed first by John von Neumann and Oskar Morgenstern, neither of whom could be described as peace researchers by any stretch of the imagination but who nevertheless made a very important contribution to the coherent theory of conflict. Perhaps it was no accident that the classic work in this field was called *The Theory of Games in Economic Behavior*.[3] Economics has a considerable structure of theory which is applicable to conflict, particularly the theory of competition among the few. Lewis Richardson's theory of arms races fits well into this pattern as I have developed it in my own book, *Conflict and Defense*.

Another important body of theory owes a good deal to Galtung. This is the distinction between associative and dissociative solutions to problems of conflict, the associative ones being such things as political organization, government, and getting people together; the dissociative ones consisting of property and "good fences make good neighbors." Both of these are important for some of the larger problems of normative science, such as what Garrett Hardin has called the "tragedy of the commons," where the absence of either associative or dissociative solutions leads to the waste of resources and everybody getting worse off. Another of these perverse dynamic processes, as I call them, is the prisoner's dilemma, studied very extensively by Anatol Rapoport and Albert Chammah,[4] in which short-run rationality again leads into positions in which everybody becomes worse off. All these are problems essentially in reducing the cost of conflict, not in winning it. If the theories

3. John von Neumann and Oskar Morgenstern, *The Theory of Games in Economic Behavior*, 2d ed. (Princeton: Princeton University Press, 1947).
4. Anatol Rapoport and Albert Chammah, *Prisoner's Dilemma: A Study in Conflict and Cooperation* (Ann Arbor: University of Michigan Press, 1965).

still seem not very well put together, we must reflect that this is the general condition of the social sciences, where general theoretical systems of society are only just beginning to emerge. Each discipline up to now has developed its own theoretical structures largely in the absence of feedback from other disciplines.

With regard to data collection and processing, considerable improvements have been made in the last twenty-five years. The Stockholm International Peace Research Institute, for instance, has been able to collect a very large amount of data on the world war industry and related topics. Professors Edward Azar and Thomas Sloan at the University of North Carolina have developed a technique for analyzing "events data."[5] This is extremely valuable in organizing the ongoing pattern of events in the international system into reasonably simple patterns. Professor David Singer and his associates at the University of Michigan have analyzed the incidence of war and peace from the beginning of the nineteenth century.[6] Professor Rudi Rummel at the University of Hawaii has developed a very elaborate factor analysis method for describing the dimensionality of nations.[7] There are many important studies of crisis patterns, and so on. There is an impressive body of empirical work, beginning with Lewis Richardson's studies on the statistics of deadly quarrels.

5. Edward E. Azar and Thomas J. Sloan, *Dimensions of Interaction: A Source Book for the Study of the Behavior of 31 Nations* (Pittsburgh: International Studies Association, 1975).
6. J. David Singer and Melvin Small, *The Wages of War, 1816–1965: A Statistical Handbook* (New York: John Wiley & Sons, 1972).
7. Rummel, *The Dimensions of Nations*.

It is always a precarious task to predict the future of research, for knowledge always has to be surprising. If we could predict what we will know in, say, twenty-five years, we would know it now. One can, however, look to the gaps in our present knowledge that may have a reasonable chance of being filled by the kinds of research we now know about. Perhaps the biggest gap is in the study of the human learning process by which our images of the world and our values are derived. An important gap here is in our knowledge of the factors which underlie the internal constraints on human behavior. As I have suggested in earlier chapters, it is very often the taboos, the things people do *not* do, that are important in creating peace, and how these internal values are set up is still very little understood. The difference between an Amin and a Nyerere is far more in their taboos, the things Nyerere refrains from doing and Amin does not, than in their positive philosophies and programs. Just what creates such an enormous change in the taboo structure when war breaks out is something I think we do not really understand.

We need many more historical studies of cases in which stable peace has been achieved. On the whole historians have been much more interested in war than in peace and indeed have tended to regard war as the normal state of affairs and peace as somewhat of an aberration. There have been enough cases now of the establishment of stable peace, however, to make careful studies of this rewarding. It may be that peace research will move somewhat out of economics, where the main problems seem not to be too difficult, and even out of sociology and political science into basic psychology, the study of learning, and history.

The final question, perhaps the most important one of all, is the extent to which peace research either has affected national policies in the past or is likely to affect them in the future. The effect in the past, it must be confessed, has been fairly small. Governments still rely on spies and diplomats for their main information with regard to the international system, in spite of the fact that this system is notoriously corrupt and is much more likely to produce misinformation than truth. Nevertheless, one can detect a certain difference in the flavor of international systems today from what they were, say, twenty years ago and much more from what they were a hundred years ago. Henry Kissinger, for instance, though his work lay somewhere beyond the margin of what we ordinarily think of as peace research, was a much more sophisticated operator in the international system than was, say, John Foster Dulles or Mr. Kellogg of the Kellogg Pact. The Vietnam War, however, demonstrated the extraordinary inadequacy of the so-called intelligence community in producing reliable information to guide government policies. Looking to the future, the current proposal in Congress, which seems to have some chance of success, for setting up a National Peace Academy might have a very significant long-run effect, similar perhaps to that of the Council of Economic Advisors, of creating an official link between the peace and conflict research community and the government decision makers. One should not expect too much of it, and there will be some fear of its being corrupted. Nevertheless, these institutional changes often introduce a bias and an asymmetry into the course of events which increase the chance that things will go from bad to better rather than from bad to worse.

The next hundred years may be the most crucial that the human race has had to face in its whole history. A major nuclear war would certainly set us back very sharply, perhaps irretrievably. The population explosion in the tropics as well as the prospect of the relentlessly rising prices for energy and materials, the possibly diminishing productivity of research, and the decline in the rate of increase of knowledge suggest that we are about to enter a period of increasing strain. In these circumstances research becomes of overwhelming importance and may make the difference between survival or catastrophe. It is well recognized that research into energy and materials, conservation and productivity, is of crucial importance if the depletion of known resources is to be offset. What is less well recognized is that the world war industry, and still more the shadow of future world war which it creates, greatly diminishes our chance of survival. One would think that research on how to diminish conflict and release these resources would have a very high priority, but unfortunately it has not. The peace research movement has always operated on a shoestring and has always been starved for funds. Our motto seems to be millions for the means of destruction but only pennies for research on how to economize them. It may take a catastrophe to awaken us to our folly. One hopes not, but we must be ready when the opportunity comes.